In the Midst

A COVID-19
Anthology

Sandy Tritt

Editor

Yellow Rose Publishing Company
Parkersburg, WV USA

A COVID-19 Anthology

Cover Art Acknowledgements

Special thanks to Lana Hunneyball for creating this unique cover arrangement. She used the layout of the card game "Patience" as a fitting representation of the patience required to get through this pandemic—and it's a form of solitaire, which is fitting since many of us are alone at this time. Isolated. Lana is a talented writer, artist, and all things creative. You can read her full bio on page 106.

The art depicted on the card faces are original art or photographs included in this anthology. A larger copy of each work, a description of the work, and a bio of the artist/photographer is found on the page number listed.

Front cover:

2 ♠ "COVID-19: Fatal Pandemic: Voice of Hope" by Tabani Mtwana (page 104)

2 ♦ "COVID-19: Novel Coronavirus" by Ayana Zaman (age 10) (page 229)

A ♥ "Learn Social Distancing from your Cat" by Sonya Gonzalez (page 113)

9 ♠ "Fishbowl – Visiting Dad" photograph by Eric Fritzius (page 63)

4 ♣ "Quarantine Went Like . . . " by Raven Berrian (age 17) (page 163)

3 ♣ "Thank You" by Crystal Brennan-Yeo and Alexa Yeo (age 10) (page 79)

K ♥ "Corona II, 2020" by Alan Grobler (page 115)

Back cover:

6 ♥ "Unexpected Turn" by Catherine de Villiers (page 3)

K ♦ "Maskmaker, Maskmaker, Make Me a Mask"
photograph by Henry Martinuk (page 20)

Q ♦ "Surviving Lockdown in Italy" photograph by George
Lies (page 77)

9 ♦ "Virus" by Erika Luzader (page 153)

Other Acknowledgements:

Many thanks to all those who helped make this anthology possible. First and foremost, this would never have happened had not so many people from all over the world submitted their work. Thank you! Next, a special thanks to the Selection Committee for their hard work and harder decisions. We received many more entries than we were able to use. Additionally, many thanks to Charlotte Firbank-King and Wilma Acree for lending their expertise in editing and advising, and to one of my oldest friends (in length of friendship, not in age—although there is some correlation there), Treva Province, for proofreading the manuscript. And more thanks to Lana Hunneyball for not only the cover design, but also for her careful proofreading and advice throughout. She was instrumental in making this into a quality production. Finally, of course, many thanks to my brilliant daughters and my patient husband for being there to advise and support.

And thank you, dear reader, for without you, nothing would be possible.

Dedication

I hadn't planned to include a dedication for this anthology, but then my long-time friend, Patsy Evans Pittman, decided to die in the midst of the pandemic and the preparation of this book. Patsy was a prolific writer who received dozens of awards and was published in respected journals, diverse magazines, and international anthologies. She also published two books, one a collection of her short stories and one a collection of her essays and poems.

Whenever I think of an anthology, I think of Patsy. I don't have a clue how many anthologies she has appeared in, but I've been surprised many times when randomly running across her name. Patsy also was instrumental in selecting and processing entries for many anthologies and literary journals. She, our mutual friend Wilma, and I often worked together. We would sometimes argue over pieces, but in the end, when we were exhausted after a long day of work, we'd come to agreement. Of course, that's when the arguments over commas began. How many word nerds can you put in one room and expect consensus?

I will greatly miss Patsy. She was the first person to encourage my writing—and who remained a loyal cheerleader—even while I admired her talents. She was a sweet person—and a power to be reckoned with. I can still hear her saying, "Oh, Miss Sandy, why did you get me involved in this?"

And my answer was always the same: "Because I love you, Miss Patsy. Because I love you."

Table of Contents

Contents by Author/Artist

Preface

You know, you should edit an anthology about COVID-19. Capture the raw emotions and coping mechanisms of people from all over the world—while the pandemic is still ongoing.

I shook my head to rid it of that crazy thought.

It came back stronger. *Millions of people throughout the world are experiencing the same emotions—anger, anxiety, fear, sadness. But they don't realize their feelings are universal—truly universal.*

I couldn't argue with that, so I ran a small ad, thinking I'd be out a few bucks and that little voice in my head would finally take a nap.

Instead, hundreds of submissions from new writers to well-published authors and from students to world-renowned artists poured in. Entries arrived from six continents (all but Antarctica!). From throughout the U.S. and Canada. From South Africa and Zimbabwe. From Australia and New Zealand. From England, Wales, Ireland, Scotland, the Netherlands. From India and Bangladesh. From Argentina. Writers and artists from ten years old to somewhere in their nineties sent poems, original artwork, fiction, essays, photographs, and scripts.

As I read, my heart ached for people suffering in so many ways from this unprecedented situation. But these entries carried much more than tears. They also showed the resilience of the human spirit. Many offered encouragement. Some shared ways of coping—especially creative ways, such as taking up new hobbies. Others found humor in the quest for toilet paper, the mandate to "wash your hands," and hair—from new hairdos and natural hair colors of those who can no longer see their hairdressers to COVID cuts for those who took the problem into their own hands. Some described new skills or practices that have improved their lives—things they will retain long after the pandemic is over. And many showed appreciation to the ones who've sacrificed to keep the world moving.

What ties them all together? The universal experience of living in isolation and anxiety during a global pandemic with no end in sight. People are in crisis and need to share their experiences and imaginative solutions.

Painstaking decisions were made to cut down the deluge of entries to this final selection of 100 pieces representing 84 authors and artists. I've always said that when you share your art or your writing, you share your soul. And we now celebrate the courageous people who have bared their souls to give you a glimpse into their lives.

While all the entries are in English, many are flavored by British spelling and punctuation, American dialect, or some combination thereof. To protect the ethnic and cultural seasoning of the contributors, we have edited with a light hand, keeping the vernacular of the country of origin. The views expressed within the entries are solely those of the contributor and may or may not reflect the views of the editorial staff.

I hope you are as touched as we have been by these honest, from-the-gut reactions while still IN THE MIDST of this historic pandemic.

Hopefully, we'll see our way out of this soon, and this anthology will become a collection to help future generations understand exactly what it was like to endure separation from friends and family, shutdowns of schools, churches, and "non-essential" businesses, and, of course, the fear and suffering caused by illness and death.

Thank you for reading. We do not expect that every entry will entertain every reader, but we are sure each reader will be profoundly affected by at least a few of the entries.

NOTE: The cover was designed and created by Lana Hunneyball. The artwork featured on the card faces are among the more than 30 original creations or photos included within the anthology.

Thank you for reading.

Sandy Tritt

IFWeditors@gmail.com

In the Midst

A COVID-19 Anthology

Unexpected Turn

Catherine de Villiers – Betty's Bay, Western Cape, South Africa

(Artwork on opposite page)

Catherine de Villiers says: "This was my COVID painting. We were under lockdown here in South Africa in March 2020. I was very aware of the fragility of mental health, with thousands of Italians dying. The songs that rose off the balconies in Italy were inspiring. A song is the universal means of communicating care.

"We were afraid. The Unexpected Turn shows the collector of souls and those who have crossed over and are in contemplation of the crossing over. The uncertainty of how to stay alive. The sureness of Death. Is it bad?"

Catherine de Villiers *is an artist and published poet who lives in Betty's Bay, Western Cape, South Africa. She is also an advocate for Children's rights and the humanitarian approach to animals, humans, plants, and her beloved ocean.*

Unexpected Turn

Catherine de Villiers – Betty's Bay, Western Cape, South Africa

The painting is 70 cm x 50 cm,
oil on very dense handmade paper.

Wrinkles

Crystal Brennan-Yeo – Goderich, Ontario, Canada

COVID has aged me.
I look in the mirror, and the lines are new.
They are deep.
This pandemic has written a story of fear across my face.
My heart. My mind.
Its tendrils slowly creep anxiety 'round my brain.
Tightening.

I can see my children.
Alone.
In their rooms.
Isolated from their friends because no one can do the math.
Ten. Ten people total. TOTAL. T-O-T-A-L.
No judgment.
Ok. Maybe a tiny bit.
But people look at me too.
Judging.
Wondering why I am so stressed.
Why don't I have a bubble? Why won't I let my kids play?
Can't I see that *they* need connection? To be social?
Yes. Yes. I know. I agree.
But count.
Your bubble is sixty, and theirs is eighty.
Not small enough. Not safe enough.
Not yet. Not for me. Not for my family.

I trace a new line, furrowed between my brow.
Blink my tired eyes, fighting the blur.
Wishing it were over.
That it never happened.
That I will wake up
And life will be as it was.

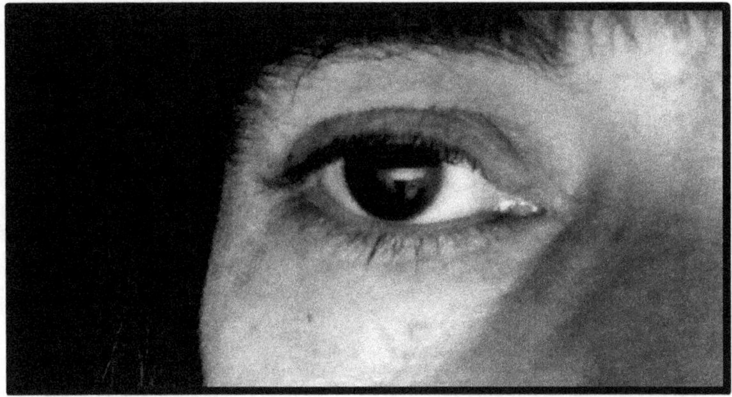

I couldn't sleep. My children were upset and missed their friends. I felt like a failure denying them. I glimpsed my reflection. I looked so old. I took this photo to see if they were real—the wrinkles that fear of COVID had recently carved deep under my tired eyes.

Crystal Brennan-Yeo loves to see language come alive through art. A teacher of Dramatic Arts, Crystal has a degree from the University of Windsor, where she found joy writing short stories, poems and plays. Her students have performed her creative scripts in competition and for community theatre. She resides in Canada.

Translation

Elizabeth Strehl – Las Vegas, Nevada, USA

The novel is more beautiful in Spanish, I've been told. It's beautiful in English, so I can't imagine what it must be like in Spanish. Even if I took the time to improve my Spanish, I would never know. The connotation would be lost. I'm not sure one can become fluent in a culture or a time or an experience not one's own.

One Hundred Years of Solitude.

Cien años de soledad.

The Spanish even sounds lonelier than the English, flowing off the tongue like a sense of longing flows from a person's eyes.

How could I have assigned *Solitude* just now?

In my defense, I had this book on the syllabus last year, taught it during these same months.

In my defense, I had this book on the syllabus from the start of this year, too. I could foresee this coming in the abstract sense, but I could not see this coming. Dystopian literature, warnings from scientists, and knowledge of history prepared me for this.

I was not prepared for this.

The Thursday before, attendance was 60%. I worked to maintain a sense of calm for my students, but inside I was fuming. I did not think school should be in session.

The dismissive kid said, "We only have one case in town."

Translation: Only one of the very few people tested has tested positive.

The dismissive kid said, "That person's kid doesn't even attend public school."

Translation: If it happens on the other side of town, it doesn't pertain to me.

What they didn't know, what I couldn't say: The man who tested positive is friends with the father of your classmate, of that girl right there. She had dinner at his house last week.

This is not to judge that kid. A month before, as the numbers in Wuhan grew, as the epidemic spread, as pandemic neared, China was that one person from the other side of town. The world was that dismissive kid.

The Friday before, attendance was 50%. I worked to maintain a sense of calm for my students, but inside I was shaking. My allergies were horrid. I couldn't stop coughing. I kept checking my forehead for a fever.

Kids grew concerned.

"Why are we here?"

Translation: I'm scared.

"Do you think we should be in school right now?"

Translation: We're scared.

"Do you think the schools should close?"

Translation: Are you scared, too?

Every kid's cough was suspect. So many coughing kids! Had I tuned it out before?

The Saturday before, I took to social media, signing petitions to close the schools, feeling the anxiety building within me.

The Saturday before, my father-in-law died. Old age, or so we thought, not yet knowing the connection between COVID-19 and blood clots. My husband made plans to go to his funeral in another state. My anxiety grew.

The Saturday before, my husband went grocery shopping alone. My cough was bad; my inhaler, insufficient. Our store had been ransacked. There was no toilet paper, no water. Most of the soup, pasta, eggs were gone. He sent pictures. I felt lucky. We don't have such a tight budget that we can't buy the more expensive brands. Those were the only brands left.

The Sunday of, I began to worry about my parents. I had last spoken to them on my father's birthday. He is seventy-seven and believed the threat wasn't real.

Sunday night, the governor closed the schools. Effective immediately and until at least April 13.

I don't think we'll be back this year.

I may never see my seniors again.

Monday, I messaged all my kids. Words of reassurance. Recommendations for living in quarantine: Set a schedule. Do your homework. Get daily exercise. Eat healthy food. Keep a journal. "Take a shower," I said. "Your parents will thank you." I wrote this unshowered, in my pajamas. I had a journal but couldn't bring myself to write in it. Instead, I was monitoring the map put out by Johns Hopkins, watching the numbers rise. I was watching the news, seeing footage from Italy, remembering my trip there in 2014. I was on Facebook sharing resources and rumors with teachers around the world. I wrote my principal, asked if we could get into the building. We left Friday not knowing we'd have no school Monday. He responded with kindness and compassion, words of reassurance. Translation: "No."

A student messaged me. She needed her psychology book so she could study. I responded with kindness and compassion, words of reassurance. Translation: "No."

Monday night, my sister-in-law decided there would be no funeral. Not yet. Funerals are for the living, and the living needed to stay alive. We'll celebrate his life once our own are more assured.

Monday night, the principal said the superintendent was allowing buildings to open. From 8:00 A.M. to 10:00 A.M., we could come in. No family permitted. No students permitted.

I arrived the next morning. It felt surreal. The principal stood at the locked door, letting us in. Our full custodial staff was cleaning the building as if it had never been cleaned before, wearing gloves and masks. I about cried.

I've been asked before what I would grab if my house were on fire. That's what it felt like when I opened my classroom door. My room was on fire. What would I grab? I took all the graded work I had yet to pass back. I could scan it for students if they wanted to see it. I grabbed books I could use to shape online lessons that actually had some meaning. I wanted to grab gifts students had given me—twenty-one years of gifts.

One student had left all her art supplies in my room, a huge box, more than I could carry out with my own crate. I stared at it, picked it up, put it down, picked it back up, moved it to a safer location. I hadn't heard from her; maybe she didn't need them. I left.

The principal's farewell should've been, "See you April 13!" It wasn't. He knew. We won't be back this year.

Wednesday, I worked from home. More email messages, posts to Google Classroom, grading. So many student concerns. I work in an International Baccalaureate Program. The central office has a COVID-19 update page. They had never canceled IB testing, not even, they said (in a boastful tone), for a hurricane or military coup. They would not cancel for a virus.

Then a student messaged me. Could she get her art supplies?

I messaged a friend. Are secretaries allowed in? Most weren't. She was, but merely to accept a delivery. She'd try.

My three cats felt my tension. All three vomited.

Wednesday, I called my parents to set my mind at ease. They were home. They were taking it seriously.

Thursday, I worked from home. The district said we'd still get paid. We needed to be working, but they couldn't tell us what to do. Not all students had computer access. I posted assignments, answered emails, graded work. I checked the numbers from Johns Hopkins and spent too much time on Facebook.

Friday, we went to my friend's to get the art supplies. She left them on the doorstep. Social distancing. We drove across town and left the supplies on the student's doorstep. She waved from afar. I went into Albertsons with my husband to get items he'd forgotten before. It was crowded. Couples with children. A shoplifter was throwing food at the security guard. There was no water, no toilet paper, no tofu. You know the apocalypse is near when tofu sells out. "You deserve hazard pay," I told the cashier. She nodded.

Friday, I messaged the kids. "Take a shower," I reminded them. I told them I would not post anything on the weekend. Weekends need to feel like weekends; weekdays, like weekdays. Translation: Nothing is normal right now, but let's pretend.

My principal messaged out. We needed to clock in and out electronically. We needed to create online assignments; we were not to grade them, though, as not all kids had access. We needed to email every kid weekly to measure "attendance." We needed to be available by email and phone from 6:50 A.M. to 2:01 P.M. Translation: Nothing is normal right now, but let's pretend.

I should journal, I thought, but I just couldn't.

Saturday, I tried to relax. Translation: I worked to keep my mind distracted.

Sunday, IB announced that exams were canceled. I heard it from students first. The announcement was sent to examiners in confidence. Translation: Share this all over social media.

Monday, I worked from home. I set my alarm, took a shower, dressed, clocked in, set up a workstation to feel official. I posted assignments, emailed students, hosted online discussions regarding *One Hundred Years of Solitude*. I did as I told the kids to do.

Welcome to my journal. I'm sure it fails to translate.

Elizabeth Strehl is an English teacher who currently works at a public school in Nevada.

Journal Entry: Pandemic

David B. Prather – Parkersburg, West Virginia, USA

My nephew tags everyone, yells *you're it*
as he touches each of us, then runs away.
                This is last year,
or five years ago, or ten. Time floods and washes away.
Today, my family is distant, an hour's drive or more,
                at the very least.
My sister orders everything online, never leaves
the house, her husband essential but working
                from home.
I've always been terrified of people. If someone
knocks on my door, I freeze and wait for them to leave.
                This could be the plague
of Athens, or Antonine, or Cyprian, or Justinian.
This could be Black Death or Yellow Fever.
                This could be The Mask
of the Red Death, which I just read again, each word,
each letter infectious. Every little ache in the body
                becomes a symptom:
heartburn, foot cramp, hangnail, bit lip.
How old is my nephew now? Last week
                he was eight.
This week he's eighteen. I can keep my distance.
I can stay away. I can sit alone for years.
                Given enough time,
I can disappear. Even the neighbors will wonder
if I'm still alive. When I emerge, I will be *it*.
                I will start all over again,
but stronger, harder to fight off,
lingering imperceptibly on the breath.

David B. Prather *of Parkersburg, WV, is the author of* We Were Birds. *He studied writing at Warren Wilson College and acting at the National Shakespeare Conservatory. His work has appeared in several journals, including* Prairie Schooner, Colorado Review, Poet Lore, The American Journal of Poetry, *and others.*

Toilet Paper

Tom Donlon – Shenandoah Junction, West Virginia, USA

You'd think this private experience would never
cause fights. It's so normal. Yet, in this pandemic,
we've taken up arms against each other. My regular
shopping trips for four mega-packs have ended.
I live with six women: my wife, four daughters,
and a lovely granddaughter. We need TP.

In April, the cashier lady said I could only have
two of the four mega-packs. Behind me in line
was a teacher for whom I had subbed. She said,
"Let me have the other two." Outside, I tried
to give $25 to her husband. They both refused
and gave me the mega-packs.

In May, I grabbed two mini-packs of TP and paid
via the self-checkout. As I bagged items, a lady said,
"You can only have one of them." "What? I've
already paid for them. I live with six women." I asked
for a manager. She arrived. "You can only have one
of them." "I've paid for them." "It is what it is, sir."

I picked up my two mini-packs and walked out.
They have me on camera, and my debit card is on file.
I expected to be stopped by the police. I got home
with no sirens. My wife called me a hero. I texted
a British cousin. She can't relate. They have bidets.
Back two days later, I wasn't thrown to the floor
or cuffed. No one bothered me. This time, I got one
mini-pack. I'm thinking of my British mother
who endured German bombs in England in WWII.
She raised us saying we should use only three sheets
of toilet paper. I never followed her instructions. I'll
shop every day if needed. Onward, TP warriors.

Tom Donlon earned an MFA from the American University in DC and was awarded a chapbook, Peregrine, in 2016 from a contest sponsored by the Franciscan University in Steubenville, OH. Poems have appeared in many journals. He has received Pushcart Prize nominations and a fellowship from the West Virginia Commission on the Arts.

Photo by Sandy Tritt

Daddy's Hands

Brian Donnell James – Manassas, Virginia, USA

As a baby
She clutched his finger tightly
And cried when he wiggled it free
And everyone knew
She was a daddy's girl
For sure

She held firm
To his hands
As she jumped puddles
Skipped and avoided sidewalk cracks
On her way to school
On her very first day

He held her close for a picture
As she looked stunning
In her prom dress
And he gave a stern eye
To her date

His hands gave her away
As wedding bells rang
But she was his little girl
Yet still

So this was the reason
She now was chosen
To hold his hands
For what might be the last time
And every time she felt the warmth leaving his fingers
She cried like a baby behind the mask
Among the sound of respirators

So he would clutch her hands tightly
This time he would not let go
No, he would not let her hand free
Because everyone knew
She was a daddy's girl
For sure

Brian Donnell James *is an emerging poet who has been published in Africa, Europe, and throughout the United States.*

All Things Considered: Life in a Pandemic

Honey Novick – Toronto, Ontario, Canada

"Hope is definitely not the same thing as optimism. It is not the conviction that something will turn out well, but the certainty that something makes sense, regardless of how it turns out." Vaclav Havel (1935-2011) former Czech president

All things considered, I'm o.k.
On Friday, March the 13th, in the morning,
my calendar was filled to October.
By Friday, March the 13th, in the evening,
only two appointments remained,
(including one dental)
cancellation after postponement after postponement,
like dominoes, one after the other,
all my work and social projects fell.
This was the start of the lockdown,
life in a quarantined pandemic.

I didn't panic. I felt as if I was, suddenly, unexpectedly,
in some kind of tsunami
and the only way out was to swim.

Like many people, I was ignorant of the oncoming pandemic.
Like some people, I went into surfer girl mode, riding the
        waves—
especially the waves of anxiety that comes with isolation—
and like some very good surfer girls, I adapted to the waves
balancing my power to the wave power
and rode them, moment by moment, wave by wave,
giving myself chores: write a daily diary,
learn a new word everyday
play the game of colours—each day find things that are
orange or green; the next day, purple, the next, etc.

sing Bob Dylan's "Lay Down Your Weary Tune"
and when the waves of fear hit,
chant, breathe, stretch, pace,
say it's o.k.
and DO NOT, EVER, think of the future, just the moment
just the NOW!

I'm told I'm in a vulnerable age group, the oldster woman,
the hippie survivor, thus, one of the ones that have to stay
    sheltered,
not going out unless it's necessary,
wash hands, don't touch face.
I don't feel I'm an oldster. I've attracted
a younger man into my life—
it's not a thing, but a realization
of my energy, life force.

I was in school when JFK was shot
I saw the Beatles change history on the Ed Sullivan Show
I heard Bob Dylan get booed when he switched from
acoustic to electric
I saw Timothy Leary tell my generation to "turn on, tune in,
drop out"—and I did.

I witnessed history unfolding—the Berlin Wall falling
the Vietnam War ending, the greed of capitalism rising
Israel, Egypt and the Palestinian Liberation Organization
together won Nobel Peace prizes
all the while I'm saying, "May we grow to understand
the harm of our ignorance."

All things considered, it is now several months of a pandemic
and I'm o.k. I feel healthy and ambitious and hopeful
and just like in the cultural revolution of the 1960s,
it was the artists, all genres of the arts, who led the way.
Now it is time to redesign and acknowledge fashions
music fashions, dancing, visuals and of course, wearables—

what to wear, how to wear what we need to wear
and especially how to be dauntless in wearing what we need
to wear like, *tada*—face masks!
The first item on the agenda.

Most of my adult life, I've worked towards bringing attention
to the older woman's visibility, viability.
It is the face that reflects images, judgments,
history, biases, warmth and reflections of oneself.
This socialist virus took it all away
making everyone's eyes the true expression of personality
giving the eyes uncommon attention and responsibility.

Marcia, my goddaughter, is a brilliant artist
using some of her time to make masks. I asked for one,
imploring, "Maskmaker, maskmaker, make me a mask,
find me a style, sew me some kinds."
She sent 3 and a bonus, her "quaranzine"
using anime creatures to emphasize
stay home, wash hands, don't touch face
get fat eating wonderful food and watching tv or some such.

When I opened the pack, I thought there may be some
mistake because these looked like men's athletic cups—
the kind that have a sort of pouch.
I was a bit reluctant to put it on my face
the implication being that I was putting a penis protector on
my nose.
I got over my trepidation quickly as the Health Officials
are constantly entreating all humans to wear masks.
I acquiesced, got rid of my imaginative musings and put it on.
Marcia's masks fit and are so well-designed
that someone commented on the beauty of the design
and the elegant craftsmanship
helping me get over my chagrin as I wore one to the
supermarket.

These masks are reversible, washable, perfectly sewn,
and, I might add, stylishly *tres chic*.
One is made from the cloth of Pooh images,
another beatnik black with tourmaline blue,
another a kind of lilac purple with flowers,
but no red as in "redress," alas.

All things considered, I'm o.k.
this is the new normal of Spring 2020.
Those of us lucky enough to have a computer
can check in with friends or zoom meetings
or sing poetry or write lyrics and pay homage
to the turning tides of the COVID-19 pandemic.
Words help, words soothe, but images
tell stories. This one honours the face mask
obliterating the facial image, yet, keeping me
and all my fellow humans safer.
All things considered, I'm o.k.
May you be o.k. and safe and smiling with that little bit of
hope safely hidden in that extra space sewn in the splendour
of your face mask.

As an afterthought, the words of Pete Seeger seem to be
timely and significant:

"Words are good, and words help us become the leading
species on earth to the point where we are now ready to wipe
ourselves off the earth. But I think that all the arts are needed,
and sports too, and cooking, food, and all these different ways
of communication. Smiles, looking into eyes directly, all these
different means of communication are needed to save this
world. But certainly a great melody . . . ."

*Honey Novick is a singer/songwriter/voice teacher/poet living
in Toronto, Canada. Her songs and poetry have been
published in Spanish, French, Urdu, and Greek. She is the 2020
awardee of the Canadian Senior Artists Resource Network
Mentor Award and has been nominated for the Acker Award.*

Maskmaker, Maskmaker, Make Me a Mask

Henry Martinuk – Toronto, Ontario, Canada

Photo of Honey Novick by Henry Martinuk

From Honey: *seeing that photo of me, my face hidden, my hat (an homage to Leonard Cohen), and the welcoming breezes of spring, gave me perspective on how fashions and health statements and even masks as political statements looked on me. It was helpful to see myself in this new world order.*

154 Days

Meg Whitlatch – Mendoza, Argentina

One hundred fifty-four days could be the number of days until something wonderful happens—counting down for graduation, a birthday, or the arrival of a new baby. It could be the number of days until my family arrives to visit me. But no, 154 days is the amount of time—one of the longest on-going quarantines in the world and not over yet—we have lived under mandatory lockdown and restrictions in Argentina.

That Saturday, back in mid-March, none of us imagined how our lives would change. Although it was a theme of conversation, none of the guests at a wedding reception were truly worried about the virus. After all, it had only spread to Europe, and only those who had travelled were at risk. Little did we know we were at one of the last weddings that would take place for many months. That Sunday, our president announced that schools were closing. Staff could still go in to prepare the buildings for returning students in the near future. Near future! Ha! That week we rushed at work to get in touch with our students, get phone lists, emails, prepare booklets with copies, and make sure we had contact numbers for all. We had just returned from summer break two weeks earlier—I still didn't know the names of my students—some I had only seen once.

But there wasn't enough time—that Thursday the president announced a mandatory national quarantine and everyone had to stay at home. Everything closed. Everyone at home. No going out to walk, no sports, no, no, no. Health and security workers were authorized, but had to show permission papers at security checks on their way to work. Grocery stores and pharmacies were also allowed to open, but the hours changed—and no more closing for siesta! And if you have ever been to Mendoza, you know no one goes to the store during siesta (nap time). But we had to adapt because stores opened later and closed earlier, and only so many people could go in at a time. Soon the province of Mendoza decided to restrict outings to the store according to the end of your ID number.

Lives were changed; everything seemed so weird. We were told what to do and what not to do. *Don't greet with a kiss on the cheek. Bump elbows instead.* Don't greet with a kiss and hug? Is that even possible here? *Don't share mate. Mate* is an herbal drink that is shared—everyone drinks from the same straw—and is a very important part of everyday life here. Not sharing *mate* is selfish—it goes against all *mate* rules. *Don't take your dog for a walk.* If you live in an apartment (like me), just take the dog out to the front sidewalk! Trust me, I was not the only one sneaking out after dark to walk around the neighborhood with my dog, keeping watch for police that may be controlling.

Don't play soccer. What on earth? How can you forbid soccer in Argentina? They closed playgrounds and taped off exercise machines. What were the kids supposed to do? *Put a container with bleach water at your doorstep for disinfecting shoes on the way in*—never mind the fact that all your pants will have a stylish white splash on them. *Have a set of clothes for outside and another for inside, take off your outdoor clothes when you arrive* (some never knew if they could change inside, so they stripped outside before entering the safe place). *Wear a face mask everywhere.*

"Don't worry," they said, "the virus isn't here. We only have imported cases."(People who were infected outside the country). "We are preparing so our medical system will be able to handle this. We expect by mid-April (then May, mid-May, and so on) we will have seen the peak and all will go back to normal." We had to be prepared. But April passed, May flew by. Birthdays, weddings, and *quinceñeras* were postponed and eventually cancelled. Tradition is that at midnight when a girl turns fifteen, her friends and family gather, throw paint and flour, and toast with her. But now, so many girls are at home without the classic *tirada*, as it's called.

June arrived, and honestly, we were all locked up in our homes, looking for some freedom and trying to understand why we were all inside with everything closed, when there were hardly any cases here. So we were allowed out for walks or bike rides, always wearing a face mask, and on the days allowed by ID number. Stores and offices slowly were authorized to open. Banks opened. Family and friend gatherings were allowed for up to ten people. Families ran to see each other after months of not being in touch. All the "don't do this or that" rules were broken, although the government repeated over and over that it was dangerous. And cases began to appear, so they decided to close some places and forbid friend and family gatherings again.

We don't have any family close enough to visit, but you see everyone sneaking around avoiding police controls in order to arrive without being caught at a relative's home. If you are caught out when not allowed or at a gathering, there are huge fines, and if they catch you more than once, you risk being sent to jail!

All seemed calm, and all those things we were told to do or not to do sometimes even seemed silly—until these past weeks. The pandemic was like an invisible threat that was not really present. It was in Buenos Aires, and it was on the other side of the mountains in Chile, but it wasn't really a big problem here. Some weeks ago, cases appeared in bigger numbers, and it became more difficult to know how someone was infected. Hospitals filled up. You should know that here anyone who tests positive is isolated in a hospital. Just recently, they decided to isolate patients with little or no symptoms in hotels, but still the ICU has more than 80% occupation.

Tomorrow is Children's Day. Usually, children would be gathering at huge celebrations in parks, families sharing *asados* and *mate* late in the evening, playgrounds overflowing, and hugs and kisses in all directions. But tomorrow will be different. No family hugs, no shared *mate* or kisses, no gatherings with friends—or at least there shouldn't be. Life has changed and we worry about going back to normal, about hugging a student or greeting a fellow teacher with a hug and kiss.

Maybe someday we will be able to share *mate* again or hug and greet each other with a kiss. Maybe someday we will be able to gather at a park for an event or see children playing in the playgrounds. Maybe someday soon we will have weddings and birthdays again. Maybe someday this will be part of history and we will say: "Remember the year when we were told to stay inside for more than 154 days?"

UPDATE (October 15, 2020)

One week later . . .

It had been cold and rainy, unusual for Mendoza. My husband Tony, an EMT, had a cold, but we figured it was the weather. His phone rang. The doctor he'd shared an ambulance with during his last two shifts had tested positive. We had to isolate. His "cold" grew worse, and two days later, a fever developed. The next day, Monday, he was tested for COVID, although we were pretty certain he was positive. I also started to present some very mild symptoms. Tony continued to get worse. By Friday evening, he couldn't breathe. We called an ambulance, and I watched him leave. Hours passed without knowing where or how he was. After midnight, I learned he was admitted to intensive care with bilateral pneumonia.

Sunday morning, his condition deteriorated. The doctors, in trying not to intubate him, connected him to a special oxygen that was introduced with pressure. He had to spend most of the time on his stomach to improve breathing. Meanwhile, I was at home sick and waiting for any little piece of news.

He received convalescent plasma transfusion later on Sunday, and slowly started to recover. On Tuesday, they gave him a second dose. He texted me. But only me. Saturday, after a week in intensive care, he was transferred to a room with regular oxygen. Slowly, they took him off medications and oxygen, and finally, on the next Tuesday, he was released after testing negative.

Today, almost a month later, he continues to stay home and rest. His lungs are still affected, but we trust all the prayers helped pull him through and will continue to help him recover.

When I wrote the original essay, I thought 154 days of isolation was ridiculous. We are now at seven months of isolation, and strong restrictions continue here. This week, we had the first flights into the country since March, but they were only for those with health issues or essential workers.

"Remember the year when we were told to stay inside for . . . the entire year?"

Meg Whitlatch *is a teacher and an interpreter living in Mendoza, Argentina. After submitting her original essay, both she and her husband were infected with COVID-19. In October, she provided the included update.*

Super Heroes

Sandy Lynn Helm Moffett – Bakersfield, California, USA

The definition of superhero has transformed—not as visibly as a toy turning into a mammoth metal warrior—but transformed, all the same.

Capes and tights have been replaced by hazmat suits and facemasks. Hands are cleaned and sanitized so many times, it's a wonder there is any skin left.

Chefs—whose exquisite food was once prepared for those who sometimes left without expressing gratitude, are now choosing to give that food free of charge to help the helpers.

Teachers—shut out of classrooms along with their students are finding new ways to touch the minds and hearts of those they have promised to educate.

Leaders in the faith community—when their houses of worship were closed, looked to untapped technology to reach and reassure their flocks.

Radio and television personalities, business owners and social media posters—decided that they would strive to remind us of the positives of life in the midst of dark days.

And lest we forget those who have vowed to protect and serve—our first responders, who as always, rush in to help, to save—even when circumstances are fraught with unknown dangers.

These people have no capes, but they are heroes none the less.

They are Super Heroes.

Sandy Lynn Helm Moffett *was born in Bakersfield, California, and returned to her hometown in 1985. She has been married to Greg for 39 years, and they have four children and 12 grandchildren. Sandy is a poet and lyricist, and has been published in* Chicken Soup for the Soul, Cup of Comfort *and numerous other works.*

We Pause this Pandemic

Sara M. Crickenberger – Lewisburg, West Virginia, USA

We pause
our regularly scheduled pandemic
to take to the streets
because we have no choice.

Wearing masks
standing six feet apart
we kneel
and raise our fists

for eight minutes and forty-six seconds
the time it takes
to squeeze the life
out of a 6-foot 4-inch Black man.

I can't breathe.

Now we return
to our regularly scheduled pandemic
to a disease that targets
those living in segregated housing

with no sick leave
or health insurance
in neighborhoods that lack food stores
and decent health care

to a disease
that sucks the life
out of Black people
four times more than whites.

I can't breathe.

Sara M. Crickenberger is the President/CEO of Carnegie Hall in Lewisburg, West Virginia. She earned her MFA in Creative Writing from Virginia Tech, where she served as the Assistant Director of the Creative Writing Program and taught writing in the English Department.

View from the Refrigerated Truck

Henry Crawford – Silver Spring, Maryland, USA

The one below me died last Thursday.
They took him to the ICU the day before.
Put him on a ventilator.

Next to me a woman I remember
from the waiting room. The steel doors opened
to a blast of sunlight and cold vapor.

Stacked her in the first
vacant space.

My wife caught me coughing.
Drove me down in our yellow Honda Civic.
She knew this woman.

They'd gone to junior high together.

There's room for another body
on my left. I saw a technician sneezing
as they were hooking up my drips.

It might be nice to see her again
but not here.

I'd tell her watch out. It's not the dying
but the dying alone. Not the pain but the
knowing. Not the void but the temperature
that gets you.

Henry Crawford is the author of two collections of poetry, American Software (CW Books, 2017) and The Binary Planet (Word Works, 2020). His online poems are available at Henry Crawford Poetry, Online. He is currently the host of the online series, Poets vs The Pandemic.

Lockdown on My Side of the Pond

Charlotte Firbank-King – Teniqua Treetops, Western Cape, South Africa

South Africa, March-August 2020:

COVID-19 takes corrupt government by surprise, briefly curtailing activities. They run about like headless chickens scrambling for ways to tackle the threat that could bring the country down. President takes bold step and just shuts the country down instead. The decision does not go down well with the majority, who live in cramped poverty.

"We suffered isolation during Apartheid, and now this?"

Powers that be find a silver lining to COVID. First logical action: ban booze and ciggies.

"Our president is controlled by that Woman Who Will Not Be Named. Her buddy is the top cigarette smuggler, and her son grows tobacco for said smuggler. The Woman and many cabinet ministers support booze smugglers as well—all good for them."

"Yeah, and our president is a nice, amiable chap who gives beautiful empty speeches, so done deal."

Official media release:

People share booze and ciggies, and tobacco is bad for your health anyway. Drunk people cause accidents and commit crimes. Our hospitals can't cope with COVID cases as it is, so certainly not alcohol-related cases as well.

Online shopping is banned. All non-essential items, like clothes, toys, and candy are banned.

"We gonna die anyway at this rate. Or kill each other."

"Who says it has to make sense?"

Smuggling trade flourishes.

"Now citizens become criminals because anyone who smokes or drinks isn't going to stop in a hurry."

Citizen protests are ignored. The Woman Who Will Not Be Named and cabinet ministers are happy as bank accounts rapidly grow. Government loses billions in tax revenue. Finance minister warns this will not end well—lifts bans. Government promises financial aid to businesses forced to shut down and the millions of people out of work as a result. Government officials steal aid money. People starve. Cigarette companies take government to court.

"At least someone is batting for us. Well, us and themselves."

President lifts ban on cigarettes. The Woman exerts pressure. President withdraws unbanning.

"She just popped his balls into her handbag."

An old law is grandly enforced: Illicit traders will be apprehended, jailed, and their contraband confiscated.

Unofficial translation:

Only smugglers not contributing to the Woman and ministers will be apprehended—their confiscated goods will be put into the hands of those "legally" contributing to the greater good—the Woman and cabinet ministers.

The armed forces are not part of the inner circle and don't know who the "legal" contributors are. Government realises that if they stop the illicit trade completely, the ministers and Woman lose out—can't have that.

Unofficial policy:

Target innocent citizens buying illicit goods, but not too diligently.

"You know what happened today? I went into a backstreet shop to buy smuggled ciggies. Three cops were outside. I smiled—they smiled. I went in and bought ciggies, then came out, ciggies hidden under other goods I had purchased. I smiled—the cops smiled—all good."

Meanwhile, the masses are still hungry and jobless. More unrest follows. The police and army are called in.

Official policy:

Anyone found congregating will be arrested.

Police brutality increases as they take the law into their own hands.

Unofficial policy:

Institute fear! It's a great way to control the masses. Target people walking on the beach with their children, or drag suspected "dissidents" from their shacks in townships and beat them up. If people are found on the street, shoot them or beat them up too. Rip children from parents' arms and toss them into childcare. That'll teach the populace to stay in their place!

Reality:

Childcare is unable to operate—funds stolen.

Food aid to starving families is stopped.

Official media release:

Food aid increases spread of COVID-19.

Reality:

Funds donated by a caring public were stolen.

"If COVID doesn't get us, starvation will."

More unrest and more force follow. In poor areas like townships, social distancing is impossible with tin shacks shoulder to shoulder and ten people crammed into a 3 x 4 m space. Domestic abuse increases.

"What about women and children seeking refuge from their abusers?"

Official media release:

No refuge permitted. It spreads COVID.

Some centres ignore COVID rules and take the poor souls in.

Official Policy:

Call in the troops—drag them from centres and force them to go home!

Abuse continues unabated—in homes and out.

Swathes of illegal squatter shacks are ploughed down along with precious belongings, leaving thousands homeless.

Official media release:

No reason.

Unable to go to school and learn or interact with their friends, kids spiral out of control. Schools aren't geared to give classes on Zoom. Not to mention, millions of kids in townships don't have access to computers, let alone internet.

"Epic fail—again."

Presidential announcement:

People must work from home.

"What? Fine if you have a computer, but how do hotel staff, builders, carpenters, and domestic helpers work from home?"

Load shedding [rolling blackouts] begins, again.

"What a mess, even those who can work from home can't. Why power outages now? Aren't things bad enough?"

Official media release:

Conductors or something malfunctioning—we think.

Reality:

Funds for maintenance have been stolen.

"Winter is coming—we can't buy warm clothing, and what about the poor people?"

Official media release:

Food and clothing donations to the poor and orphanages banned. It spreads the virus.

"Hypothermia or starvation will get us if COVID doesn't do the job."

"I need a drink."

---END OF REPORT---

I know many countries are in similar positions, but is it as bad as in my beloved country?

I live with my family at Teniqua Treetops Lodge—not operating, of course. Ergo, no income, and staff laid off. We collected funds from neighbours and bought food parcels— which entailed sneaking it to our staff—no name for that sort of criminal activity.

We're surrounded by beautiful indigenous forests and wildlife. I'm incredibly blessed in comparison.

Four months into lockdown, I haven't seen our gate to the main road about a kilometre away—my age puts me at risk. Great! My kids do my shopping, and I get to see them whenever I want. Besides, being a recluse is what I do best, and I hate shopping—all good.

Or so I thought.

Now I want to go shopping—see if we still have a world out there—sorry for me.

Reality check. I have a roof over my head, go to sleep in my nice warm bed and have a meal every day—but millions don't have this privilege. How can I not feel for them—not feel helpless and guilty?

On a lighter note: My German shepherd has a routine. Every day, fifty times a day, whenever there's the slightest sound out of the ordinary—"ordinary" being silence except for wind blowing through trees, guests walking by, or animal sounds like birds, chickens, goats, and horses—he charges from the cottage to see what's going on.

Now, we only have wind and animal sounds. But, hey, he still gets to bark at occasional cars or neighbours walking to their properties along the servitude—bonus if they're walking their dogs.

Difference is, I now understand why—he's fenced in—isolation.

The highlights of his weeks were going with me in the car on shopping expeditions. But I'm in isolation, so his isolation has increased.

We walk a few meters to my studio, where he gets to chase monkeys and I get to disappear into my art, a huge fairy painting. Or we have family dinner evenings, and he can interact with the kids and their five dogs. The dogs can compare notes on what they saw today or how many monkeys they chased.

The odd thing is, after five months into lockdown, I also jump up to see who or what he's barking at.

I haven't caught myself barking at monkeys, cars, or people yet, but it's tempting.

Charlotte Firbank-King *is the author of numerous books—mostly historical romance, but also a few for young adult and children—four of which are published. In addition, she's an editor and ghostwriter for Inspiration for Writers, Inc. Charl lives in South Africa on part of the Outeniqua forest in the Western Cape.*

Fairy Painting

Charlotte Firbank-King– Teniqua Treetops, South Africa

This is just a portion of the 1.3 x 1.1 m fairy painting Charl worked on during the COVID-19 lockdown. "Painting is my happy place where I can disappear into a fantasy world of fairies, unicorns, dragons, and elves," she says. Copies of this painting will be available as a 2500-piece puzzle.

Charlotte Firbank-King's *paintings have been sold and exhibited throughout the world and have been commissioned by the Johannesburg Zoo, the Witwatersrand National Botanical Gardens, and the Zulu Schools Trust, among others. She lives in South Africa on part of the Outeniqua Forest in the Western Cape.*

COVID-19

Anke Hodenpijl – Bakersfield, California, USA

The doctor checks my labs
"Good to go," she says
I breathe with relief,
eager to escape this breeding ground—
doorknobs, pens, magazines, chairs,
even the toilet paper—hosts for the enemy

I push the door with my derriere
like a quarterback.
I backpedal
dodge the incoming person
and veer to my Honda

Antiseptic towels at the ready,
hands sanitized,
I sing my twenty-second song,
claim a virus-free victory

What's that under my car?

a red wallet.

I scrub it with antiseptic,
(crush those pathogens)
a drivers license falls out

it belongs to Edna
I am sure she is inside that booby-trapped office
a fellow patient,
behind all those hazards
fodder for my new-found anxiety

my options play in slow motion
look to the right
look to the left
the lot is empty
no receiver to take the pitch

I.   Go.   Back.

Is Edna here?

Anke Hodenpijl says: *Poetry is the only way I have of sorting things out. I create using Indo-Dutch eyes, immigrant ears, minority strength, open arms, and a beating heart. I uncover wisdom that only writing can give me and get excited when I can share these words with the world.*

Back to the Real World

Sophranitis (14 years old) – Pietermaritzburg, KwaZulu-Natal, South Africa

Is this the turnoff? My body tenses automatically. But no, it must be the next one. Strange to have forgotten already. I'm smoothing the hem of my skirt, tapping Morse code messages on my knees. It feels like the very first day all over again. Part of me can't quite believe I'll still have the friends I made in January. Alex didn't reply to my last text message . . . .

We turn into the gate and slot into a parking space. Dad tells me to get a move on, but I feel reluctant to leave the safety of the car. *This is ridiculous!* I tell myself. *You've been aching to come back all lockdown.*

After extensive sanitizing and COVID screening, I go, as instructed, to the rugby field and anxiously scan the assembled faces for someone I know. Not many people have arrived yet, but even in a crowd it would be hard to miss Julia's hair. She and Candice seem to be doing a TikTok dance and giggling. I hesitate a moment, unsure of my welcome. These are the cool kids. I'm not quite one of them . . . .

But Alex grins at me and waves, and I run over, narrowly missing a prefect. Oh, well, he never was much of a chatter on WhatsApp.

Julia is talking about some new boy who's moved in next door, Morten's telling Ivan about Formula 1 racing, Candice is complaining about how thin her tights are—"But, oh, aren't the pants awful!" They pause to acknowledge my presence, then carry on talking. That's okay. I'm one of the group. I always was more Alex's friend than Candy's.

The school grounds have been covered in meticulously painted dots, all precisely 1, 5 metres apart. Alex has the next one along; Candy and the others are farther down. Cath hasn't arrived yet, but I'll try to save her a space. Erik is still snoozing in his room at hostel and won't wander in until ten minutes before the bell. Alex is chatting nineteen to the dozen, mostly less-than-flattering Candice anecdotes. Can't be easy having a twin.

I tell him about lockdown exercise and extra maths, and he grins at me so that dimples appear underneath his eyes. He smiles at me more now. I suppose it feels safer when Lacy's not around. It's nice not to be glared at every time I speak to him, so I can't drum up much sadness about her absence. I really must try to be charitable and feel sorry she's now on her own.

"Soph, are you listening?"

I start guiltily. "Yes, of course. Sorry!"

"Nah, you're not, but that's fine. Say 'hi' to Lacy. I've got her on video call."

"Oh, er, hi, Lace!"

Is he psychic?

Sophranitis is 14 years old and lives in South Africa. She wrote this piece shortly after returning to school after being home for four months of lockdown.

Down Under

Martin Chivaku – Harare, Harare, Zimbabwe

He coughed, his temperature sat
On the summit, sneezed, had a headache
Among many and he was taken away
From us—we cried—but didn't
Return for us to touch or
Feel but just a
Gazunder,

For the price our hearts had to
Offer—

The world played peekaboo and
We didn't receive a clear conscience
As compared to what we had opted for
From the Genesis of our prophesied
Redemption.

Perhaps, it's just a virus that'll
Disappear into time and I'm not
Supposed to worry because even
Without the shadow of doubt,
Redemption is coming—

But tell that to the empire
That succumbed to the ravages
Of its atrocities,

And give me a call when you're done.

A proclaimed conspiracy—perhaps—to
Give the sense of hate amongst our
Clear conscience and fight, fight,

Fight each other when like
Bugs in a fumigated room
We're hitting the
Ground,

For an emotional
Cause.

We can smell the end as we
Are slowly falling into blue and black
But for a happy ending cause,
We'll bump into an
Antidote—

And be free from
The virus.

Martin Chivaku of Zimbabwe is renowned as the first Zimbabwean poet to write a hundred poems in a hundred days. He's made friends with fellow poets globally and had a few poems published on poetryxhunger.com. He was invited to the Bridgewater International Poetry Festival.

Sitting in the Park

Johann Opperman – Pretoria, Gauteng, South Africa

During the cloudy and gloomy days of COVID-19, I have spent much alone time walking, moving, dreaming, breathing, observing, and sketching. In public parks, I have encountered aged, lonely, and desperate souls who inspired my charcoal and PITT pencil drawings. They are gazing at a frightening world and a bleak future. Let us breathe together.

Johann Oppermann *matriculated in 1979 from the Pretoria Art, Ballet, and Music School. He obtained a master's degree in Fine Arts (1999, University of Pretoria) and a PhD (History of Art) (2013, University Free State.) He is a graphic artist who has partaken in several local and international art exhibitions.*

Letter to the Left Behind (fiction)

Henry T. Ireys – Paw Paw, West Virginia, USA

My Dear Children:

Through the windows of my hospital room, I could see you mouthing words of love, pained faces wondering what to do and where to go. Watching me die was not easy and each of you, I know, suffered in your own particular way. I write this letter to help dress the wound of witnessing my death and perhaps to fill, in part, the void that follows a parent's final exit.

The virus that killed me is a mystery. I don't mean a biological mystery or a public health mystery or even a political mystery. Of course it's all those things, and will be for a while longer. But it's also a spiritual mystery. Why did I die, healthy and vigorous until I wasn't, while your grandmother lived on with her asthma and diabetes? Is there meaning to my death?

Your presence, even from a distance and even when it could only be occasional, was important. And so I write also to thank you for your willingness to bear witness, to return often to that window despite the difficulty of looking through it. You could not know with certainty that you did not need to do or say anything. Your presence was enough.

Before the virus struck, I fancied myself free because I was healthy. But an illness robs a person of certain liberties, just as a pandemic robs society of certain freedoms. Of course, when the ultimate thief arrives to threaten whole families and communities, survival replaces freedom as the most urgent issue.

And so I survived for a while, connected to the electric version of a humming whirligig with fluctuating fluorescent lines and flashing numbers. At the end, it allowed the nurse to note my time of death. Tidy, precise, irrevocable.

Dylan Thomas urges us to "not go gentle into that goodnight . . . To rage, rage against the dying of the light." His wish to grasp life and hold on at all costs appealed to me for most of my life. But in the few days before my death, not so much. A ripe stoicism prevailed over any romantic impulse. Or maybe the fierce fire of my determined struggle to live an interesting life had burned down to a winking ember of simple acceptance. In any case, I saw no need for rage. That you all stood smoldering in frustration against the mystery of the virus, against the imperatives of caution, was something I could do nothing about.

Just like I could do nothing about the conflicts and troubles each of you is facing as a so-called adult. Tough relationship problems. A shuttered economy. A deeply troubled world. I suppose I was not much help to you in the last few years. I'm not sure I even wanted to help after all the grief you delivered when you were teenagers. *Those* were problems. Belligerence. Poor judgment. Arrogance. Alcohol-fueled risk-taking that I didn't want to know about. Friends with signs over their heads flashing "trouble" in big red letters that somehow you missed. I realize you were just growing up, but that doesn't mean I forgive you for any of it.

Anyway, being your father, I can't resist making a few suggestions in the probably misplaced hope that they will rescue you from some future agony. So here it is, the post-death deathbed advice: Have faith in love, but keep searching hard for understanding. An enduring commitment to someone else brings discomforting discoveries about yourself, but it's still worth it. Solutions emerge from imaginative reflection, but you've got to give it some time. OK, dad's done. No use going on and on when you've stopped paying attention.

Near the end, you watched through the window as I lifted my scrawny, withered hand in a gesture of recognition. In my mind, each of you clasped on. I *felt* your hands as if they were touching me in truth. Your hands were there, *really*. Deep comfort. Such is the power of love.

I couldn't hold my arm up for long. It just fell slowly to my chest all on its own. After a few minutes, the nurse made her note. You all turned away.

Death brought a surprising benefit: I could clearly see the near future. It turns out that your mother will be joining me soon. The virus again. Even quicker. She won't suffer long, and that is good. And we'll be together again for a while. That's good too. The freedom to argue with her has been one of those liberties I've missed the most.

You will be left behind, but you will cope. And I can see that the virus—its haunting deaths and lingering sorrows— will be a crucible for each of you to become more of who you are already. For the artists among you, it will invite new work; for the engineers, new solutions; for the nurturers, more compassion than ever. And then, one day, it will be over. The masks will disappear. You will hug your friends without worry. The forgetting will begin quickly.

For now, whatever meaning our deaths may have will be yours to invent. How will you choose to fill the void? Your mother and I will be watching.

With everlasting love,

Dad

P.S. Okay. I forgive you.

__Henry T. Ireys__ lives and writes on his farm in Hampshire County, West Virginia.

Lockdown Limericks

Joani Geldenhuys-Jenkins – Durban, KwaZulu-Natal, South Africa

1. In Level Five of lockdown,
    The economy started to drown.
    Some folk got quite lazy
    Others stir crazy,
    Coz no-one could go into town.

2. There was a young girl named Mpho,
    Who in lockdown, just started to draw.
    She used stacks of paper,
    And danced a cute caper,
    When a publisher knocked at her door!

3. There was a nice woman called Suze,
    Who spent lots of money on booze.
    With the alcohol ban,
    Became an orange juice fan,
    And spent the saved money on shoes.

4. There was a young fella called Cyrus,
    Who contracted the Coronavirus.
    His wife was amazed,
    That he wasn't fazed,
    And listened all day to the wireless!

5. There was an old dude name of Stokes,
    Who was clearly in love with his smokes.
    The cigarette ban,
    Made him a touchy man,
    And he frightened a number of blokes!

6. There was a kind lady named May,
    Who made some dessert every day.
    She went into the 'hood,
    Sharing some pud,
    To keep COVID boredom at bay.

7. There was a young woman called Ling,
    Who wanted a nice lockdown fling.
    She decided Corona,
    Would simply not own her,
    So she started to dance and to sing!

8. There was a sweet lady called Liza,
    Who bought plenty of hand sanitiser.
    Kept a hundred and ten,
    Bottles stashed in her den,
    But no-one was any the wiser!

9. A creative woman called Pat,
    In lockdown, just never got fat.
    She ate healthy food,
    Improving her mood,
    In view of her yoga mat!

10. There was a fit fella called Ace,
    Who loved nothing more than to race.
    He ran on the spot,
    And worked out a lot,
    In his lockdown exercise space.

11. The global Pandemic hit hard,
    Health Care Workers were ever on guard.
    Worked hours each day,
    To chase COVID away,
    Despite this, some lives were still scarred.

12. Masks, clean hands, and distancing,
    Became a familiar ring,
    As the virus went wide,
    COVID kept us inside,
    For a new-normal life to begin.

Joani Geldenhuys-Jenkins loves the magic of language and the wonderful world we can escape to through the written word. She's a former English and Drama teacher, retired Methodist Minister, Freelance Marriage and Family Counsellor, Motivational Speaker, Retreat and Workshop leader. She lives in South Africa.

Maungawhau Lockdown Haiku

Paige Turner – Auckland, New Zealand

"Will freedom return?"
asks the ancestral mountain
"Yes," sing the songbirds

12 August 2020: Lockdown. Auckland, New Zealand: I hear peaceful birdsong while lockdown-walking to the crater of *Maungawhau* (Mt Eden), my adopted *Tipuna Maunga* (Ancestral Mountain). Why's there a massive traffic jam in the city below? Businesses are closed. Everybody's working from home. Oh! It's people queuing for COVID-19 tests.

Paige Turner is a writer who likes to keep her readers guessing right up until the last page. In a global pandemic, she turns to poetry, surprising even herself. She lives in a city full of ancestral mountains. This haiku was written on one of them—Maungawhau/Mount Eden in New Zealand.

Fishbowl (a 2020 Monologue)

Eric Fritzius - Lewisburg, West Virginia, USA

SETTING: The exterior of a nursing home/rehabilitation facility, small town Mississippi, late March 2020.

Blank stage.

SON, mid-40s, tired, enters. As he approaches center, SON begins looking toward an imaginary 6'x6' bay window, located down stage center. He approaches it as if peeking around the corner of the edge of the window into a smallish room beyond. SON spots his DAD and smiles. (DAD is unseen and unheard by audience, but his dialogue is represented below, in CAPITALS, for timing and context purposes. Only SON's dialogue should ever be heard.)

SON
(SON dials on cell phone. Puts it to ear. SON nods to DAD beyond glass. Unseen, DAD isn't swiping to answer his own phone, which is frustrating to SON. Speaking loudly to be heard through glass) You have to answer it, Dad. *(Makes a swiping motion over phone screen to demonstrate.)* No. No, Dad, you have to swipe it. *(Makes swipe again.)* Swipe . . . . No. Swipe it! Press harder. *(Smiles.)* Yeah. There. *(Phone to ear.)* Hey.

DAD
SORRY.

SON
Still getting used to the new phone?

DAD
DADBLAMED THING. WHAT WAS WRONG WITH MY OLD PHONE?

SON
Your old phone didn't work, Dad, that's what was wrong with it. The new one will be fine. You just have to get used to the touch screen.

DAD
I MISS HAVING BUTTONS.

SON
The new one *has* buttons. They're just virtual.

DAD
AND I KEEP PRESSING THE VIRTUAL BUTTONS AND NOTHING HAPPENS!

SON
Press with intent, Dad. Remember how I showed you? Ask any one of the nurses in there and they'll be able to help. *(Beat)* Don't ask Silent John. Or anyone else your age, for that matter. *(Realizes he may have gone too far.)* Sorry.

DAD
HOW YOU DOING?

SON
I'm doing . . . all right. A little bit stressed. How about you?

DAD
JUST GLAD TO SEE YOUR FACE.

SON
Glad to see your face, too, Dad, even if it has to be through your window.

DAD
I'M LIKE A FISH IN A FISHBOWL IN HERE. DON'T TAP ON THE GLASS.

SON

(Nods along, then in unheard unison . . .) "Don't . . . tap on the glass." Yeah. You told me that one yesterday.

DAD

I DID? WELL, BLAME YOUR MOTHER FOR NOT BEING HERE TO STOP ME.

SON

How's your physical therapy coming?

DAD

GREAT! LOOK HOW MUCH I CAN MOVE MY RIGHT FOOT NOW!

SON

I see that. That's a lot more movement than last week. You'll be back on your feet in no time.

DAD

I THINK THEY'RE GONNA LET ME OUT OF HERE.

SON

Well, I . . . *(Looks away, nervous.)* I wouldn't get my hopes up on coming home just yet, Dad. Even without the virus, it's not safe for you. Your therapists say you need more time or you'll always be in danger of falling. Spinal surgery is a serious thing to recover from. That's why I came down here to help out. *(Holds hand up above eyes to block the glare and squints to see something through glass.)* Hey, was that the Bird Lady I just saw go by?

DAD

HUH?

SON

Your fellow resident—the one I called Bird Lady. I thought I saw her scooting past your doorway in her wheelchair.

DAD
PROBABLY WAS. SHE GETS AROUND.

SON
I thought all the residents were supposed to be confined to their rooms, like you?

DAD
CAN'T CAGE THAT BIRD.

SON
(*Laughs.*) That's a good one. "Can't cage that bird." I'll have to remember that when I write my COVID Lockdown memoir. (*Beat*) Bird Lady's the best. She still doing the bird calls day and night? "Hu hooo."

DAD
NO. SHE'S BEEN A QUIET BIRD THIS WEEK.

SON
Yeah… Not much to sing about, I guess. I'm amazed I saw her at all. I can barely see you through the glare on the window.

DAD
I'M LIKE A FISH IN A FISHBOWL IN HERE. DON'T TAP ON THE GLASS.

SON
(*Nods along with each of DAD's words, then in unheard unison*) " . . . in here. Don't tap on the glass." Yeah. You told me. (*Awkward pause.*) Did you, uh, see the pictures Elaine sent? Of the assisted living facility she's found out near her. In Texas?

DAD
DON'T THINK SO.

SON

Oh? I'll get her to text them to you again. I think you and Mom will really like the place. Unfortunately, it's on lockdown, too. They probably won't accept new residents again until the number of COVID cases in Texas drops. Seems like that might be a while, Texas being so . . . big, and all.

DAD

AND HOT.

SON

True. And hot. *(Beat)* I've, uh . . . I've been talking to Lee Ann Joseph—you know, the real estate agent with her picture on all the grocery carts? She says she doesn't think we'll have any trouble selling the house once we get a few things brought up to code. She's been trying to get an electrician to come take a look. Not sure how safe that would be—what with Mom's lung condition and how things are going out here.

DAD

AND HOW ARE THINGS GOING—OUT THERE?

SON

Hm? Well, things still pretty much suck, and no one's real clear on when the sucking's going to stop. New states are reporting COVID cases every day. Only three back home in West Virginia, thankfully, but we're up to 17 here in Mississippi. Everybody is supposed to be staying at home—practicing "social distancing," they call it. Nobody but essential workers are supposed to be out and about. Anything that could constitute a gathering has been canceled. No concerts. No weddings. No church. No movies. No sports period—all the hosts on ESPN look like they're about to cry.

DAD

I'VE SEEN THEM. IT'S HEARTBREAKING.

SON
(Laughs) Yeah, they are pretty pitiful. *(Beat.)* Restaurants were also told to close. They can do takeout, but no dine in. I guess things must really be serious, cause they closed all the bars too.

DAD
BARS DOING TAKEOUT?

SON
No. The bars are not doing takeout. But apparently the liquor stores have been declared as essential businesses, so they're cleaning up big. Not that I would know.

DAD
TELL `EM TO SEND A FEW BOTTLES OUR WAY. WE COULD SURE USE SOME IN HERE.

SON
(Laughs.) I bet you could use some. I don't know how they expect you to stay confined to your rooms without booze.

DAD
WE LIVE IN CHALLENGING TIMES.

SON
(Squints, then points at something through glass, in unseen hallway beyond.) Oh, hey . . . they caught her. I just saw a nurse wheeling Bird Lady back past your door. They've got the staff in there all masked and gloved up, too, I see. At least they're taking it seriously. *(Beat.)* "Hu hooo."

DAD
CAN'T TELL ANY OF THEM APART ANYMORE.

SON
I guess it would be hard to tell anyone apart. But just know they're wearing the masks for your protection. It's why this

place went on lockdown last week. We don't want anything like what happened at that nursing home in Seattle . . . *(Stops. Long pause.)*

DAD
WHY? WHAT HAPPENED IN SEATTLE?

SON
Never mind. We just want you safe. *(Paces.)* It's weird out here, Dad. I remember when Elaine and I were kids, the weather guy only had to whisper the words "possible flurry" and the grocery stores would instantly be cleaned out of bread and milk—as if we were going to be snowed in for weeks in northeast Mississippi. *(Beat.)* It's like that in the stores now, except it's for Lysol, hand-sanitizer, bleach, and toilet paper. Whole aisles, just . . . gone. Made me thankful that mom forgot to turn off the Amazon subscription to Cottonelle for the past three months. We literally have 192 rolls of toilet paper at home right now.

DAD
SHE'S A WISE WOMAN.

SON
She is a wise woman, indeed. *(Sighs.)* We're trying not to let things get us down too much. Well . . . I am, anyway. Mom mostly just stays in bed, watching CNN. I keep trying to get her to at least watch something happy, but it's hard to pull her away from the President's news conferences. She . . . she hates that little orange man with a passion.

DAD
THAT SHE DOES.

SON
He'd better be glad she's on oxygen and can't drive, 'cause D.C. is not far enough away to stay her wrath. The only thing that calms her down are ice cream bars, so I've kept us in stock

on those in our weekly Kroger delivery. I've been avoiding stores myself and staying home. I can't risk getting sick and bringing it back to Mom. But I still figured coming out to see you here was essential business too, even if it's only through the window.

DAD
I'M LIKE A FISH IN A FISHBOWL IN HERE. DON'T TAP ON THE GLASS.

SON
(Nods, repeating in unheard unison.) "I'm like a fish in a fishbowl in here. Don't tap on the glass." *(Resigned.)* Yeah, Dad. You told me. *(Looks up and inhales a sudden breath.)* This is so hard, Dad. This was already hard before the virus. Now it's so much . . . bigger. It's like all my—our—problems are magnified by the pandemic, and all the plans I'd made for getting you guys into assisted living are just dreams. I mean, I know I'm where I need to be. I don't regret being here. But the whole world is in turmoil, and Stephanie and the kids are all back home going through it without me. I have no idea when I'm going to be able to see any of them, outside of a chat screen. No idea when I'll even set foot in West Virginia again . . . *(Hears a buzz and looks at phone.)* Hold on, Dad. It's Lee Ann Josephs calling. Might be about the electrician. I'll call you back in a minute. *(Swipes phone. Turns profile away from window.)* Hey, Lee Ann.

LEE ANN
AARON. I WAS ALREADY GOING TO CALL YOU ABOUT THE HOUSE, BUT NOW THERE'S SOMETHING ELSE . . . .

SON
Sure. What's up?

LEE ANN
HAS THE NURSING HOME CALLED YOU?

SON

No, the nursing home hasn't called. But I'm there, now. Why?

LEE ANN

YOU HAVEN'T SEEN THE NEWS ON TV?

SON

No. What was on the news?

LEE ANN

OH, AARON. WCBI JUST SAID THERE'S BEEN A CASE OF COVID-19 REPORTED THERE.

SON

(Turns to look through window.) Reported here?

LEE ANN

YES. ONE OF THE RESIDENTS HAS IT. I DIDN'T KNOW IF YOU'D HEARD, BUT THOUGHT YOU'D WANT TO KNOW.

SON

Yeah . . . Shit. Um. Sorry, for the cussin'. I'm just—*(Suddenly realizing.)* Oh, my god. I've got to get home and tell Mom before she hears about it on TV. And Dad. What do I even tell Dad?

LEE ANN

I'M SO SORRY, AARON. CAN I DO ANYTHING?

SON

No. No, thanks for calling me. Goodbye. *(Hangs up. Starts to walk away, then stops, remembering his dad. SON turns back to look in the direction of the window. SON moves back in front of the window, looking DS through it, and dials on cell phone.)* No . . . No, Dad, you have to swipe it! *(Mimes swiping. Swiping gets rapid and angry. Suddenly nearly in tears. Under breath.)* Just swipe it, goddammit. *(Pause. Raises phone to ear. Takes a moment to compose self.)* Hey. Dad, I have to, uh . . . I have to go. I have to make some phone calls, all right? Just . . . do me a favor . . . *(Beat.)* Close your door. Close it and keep it closed at all times, okay? It's important. *(Nods.)* I'll call you later. I . . . I love you, Dad.

DAD
I LOVE YOU TOO, SON.

SON lowers phone and hangs up. He stares through the window for a good four Mississippi Waves. Starts to exit, then stops and looks up at the sky, sniffing sharply. SON turns and exits SL, raising phone to begin dialing as he goes.

END

Eric Fritzius lives in Lewisburg, West Virginia, where he's an audio book narrator and freelance creative type. His short plays have been performed across northern Appalachia and occasionally north of the Mason-Dixon too. His fantasy collection, A Consternation of Monsters, *is available in a variety of formats.*

Photo, next page, by Eric Fritzius, entitled, "Fishbowl—Visiting Dad"

Eric says, "In March 2020, my father, Robert, was doing in-patient rehabilitation following spinal surgery. When COVID-19 hit, all visitations were restricted to windows only. During one, I noticed that Dad was perfectly framed within my own masked reflection, and I snapped the photo. This became daily reality for nursing homes in 2020."

COVID Chaos

Angia Thomas Hughes – Charleston, West Virginia, USA

The news,
The stories,
The data,
Chaos invaded
My space.

My peace,
My joy,
And contentment
Displaced.

The stores,
A madhouse,
Their shelves
So strangely
Barren.

The office,
The business,
Shut down,
And working
From home.

People,
All distanced,
Streets so empty,
I feel
So alone.

The virus,
It creeps,
It breathes,

A force new,
Unknown.

The doctors,
The nurses,
Work and toil,
Day in,
And out.

Minutes turn
To hours
And days without end.
What could we have done
So it didn't all begin.

Angia Thomas Hughes *was born and raised in West Virginia, and resides in Charleston with her humble hound Sophie. Angia's hobbies are varied. Her greatest passions are family, faith, and writing. "If what I write touches one person in some way, the effort was not wasted."*

The Wooden Stool: Creativity during a Pandemic

Dr. Monolina Bhattacharyya-Ray and Sumedha Ray (age 14)
– Hamilton, Ontario, Canada

Before the pandemic lockdown started, it was March Break. For a teenager and her mother, any break is a challenge. My own plans would never coincide with my daughter's—I knew that very well. In the stream of arguments and disagreements, the break would pass; little, if any, would be achieved. I don't want to sound like a mean mother—I was happy to give her extra sleep time and relax the discipline that comes with a break from the daily routine of middle school and after-school activities.

With the extra time added on due to the impending pandemic, I had something in mind. For many years, I had a bunch of ugly folding tables lying in my basement. I wanted to spruce them up but never found the time. This was the perfect opportunity. When I broached it with my daughter, she agreed. She is a good artist. And she loves to work with me on art projects.

Being an art historian, I can visualize artwork that would be both eye-catching and culturally meaningful in my house. As a starter, I picked the small round stool with metal legs as an experiment in art. As a theme, I chose the owl, a personal favorite. From where I emigrate, West Bengal, India, the owl is an auspicious bird: a personal vehicle of Lakshmi, the goddess of Wealth, the owl is a harbinger of good fortune.

The owl is a popular figure in the West as well; it is associated with wisdom and vigilance, with its association as such going back to the days of Ancient Greece. The presence of an owl is significant in many Eastern cultures, such as a symbol of luck in Japan. However, the owl is a symbol of death and a harbinger of bad omen in the indigenous cultures of

North American tribes. During Halloween, owls are believed to accompany witches.

The owl has featured ubiquitously in the art of Bengal, particularly its folk arts and crafts, in many creative ways. Wooden owls have now become the symbol of Bengal handicrafts. A whole village named Nutangram in Burdwan District of West Bengal specializes in this craft of producing painted owls from a single piece of wood. From very tiny to life-size, from brightly colored to plain varnished, from intricate designs to plain lines, these owls definitely are decorative objects that brighten up any room. Be it free standing, attached to a lampstand, or even as jewelry, the owl is an extremely popular item that has made its way from a small village in Bengal to being a product of the intangible cultural heritage of India.

My daughter and I had always been fascinated by these owls. They fit both our Indian heritage as well as our present context of living in North America. They offer the perfect framework for the creative mind to wander in imaginative ways through free-flowing designs and colors. We decided to give it a try on this ugly stool.

And we are very happy with the end product that brightens up a corner of the house. Most importantly, this project gave my Canadian-born daughter a chance to explore a part of her heritage. Through a combination of learning and art, this project gave us excitement and something creative to work on, taking our minds off the anxiety and uncertainty of the pandemic situation we are currently in. And it made us look forward to more creative ventures within the house. Think creative; look around; you will find things to do; your tools are right in front of you.

Sumedha at work

Sumedha and Monolina are a daughter-mother team who love to engage in creative work, mostly art. *Sumedha* is a Grade 9 student who paints mostly in acrylic and watercolor. Her mother, **Dr. Monolina Bhattacharyya-Ray,** is an art historian who is passionate about folk arts and crafts, particularly from India. Dr. Ray wants to ensure that with projects such as these, daughter Sumedha will develop knowledge of her Indian artistic heritage and will try her best to showcase them in whichever way possible.

Bread in Hand

Hiram Larew – Churchton, Maryland, USA

But even after all of this
        farmers keep farming
        for every one of us
They bend the sun
        and raise the earth
        each day for us
They round each rough
        and tamp down these fears
        for each of us
Yes after all of this
        They're the songs of life for us

And even after all of this
        the grocers pickers baggers stackers sorters drivers
        checkers
        and sweepers too
        are here for us
Like bowls of life
        they give us each our every day
        and so renew that sense of trust for us

And even after all of this
        and just as much
        are those who volunteer to serve the soup
The ones who help and give and care on our behalf
Their hands and hearts
        shape our thanks—
No matter what else happens
        they are life itself for us

And yes even after all of this
These days seem like troubled fields to us
    with deep shadows across the views
    but with growing hopes there too
        surrounding all of those who stand and wave
        bread in hand
        through all of this

Note: This poem first appeared on the Poetry X Hunger website (PoetryXHunger.com)

Hiram Larew's *poems have appeared widely and have been nominated for four Pushcarts. His Poetry X Hunger initiative is bringing poets to the anti-hunger cause. On Facebook at Hiram Larew, Poet and at Poetry X Hunger.*

We Are All in this Together

Ger Duffy – Waterford, Ireland

Ask for an appointment in the children's clinic,
eyeing the crosshatched pattern on her girl's right thigh,
lines intersecting, undercutting each other,
some light, others separating flesh, the crusts red,
her urgency is not theirs. Take her to A&E
or stay at home and wash your hands.

Wait twelve months for a prostate biopsy. Even if we could
give him an appointment, no samples are being tested,
no tests are being analysed. Nothing, in fact, can be done.
It's really bad timing to have cancer. Let's hope
the tumour stays localised. Tell him to stay at home and
wash his hands.

She types *Home Maker,* lists her hobby as baking.
She sets up a "Go Fund Me" page, the kids in best clothes,
smiling for Santa as if it's Christmas Eve. She orders
Christmas from Argos in May. The cancer is in her collar
bones, stage 4, her palliative drug unavailable from the HSE.
At night she smokes until she is stoned.

We are all in this together. Stay at home and wring your
hands.

.

Ger Duffy *is a writer living in Waterford, Ireland. Her short fiction and poetry have been published by* Slow Dancer Press (UK), The Women's' Press (UK), *and* The Viking Press (UK). *Her drama has been performed in the UK (the Albany Empire Theatre) and published by Sheffield University Press.*

Alone, Not Gone, Not Yet (fiction)

George Lies – Morgantown, West Virginia, USA

Adjusting alone has been tough, but got used to existing in a mired condition. Want to yell out loud at times, find myself not in line with changes that make no sense. I feed the birds bread, watch from a kitchen window; the claws squeeze branches until orange Obie or fluffy Douglas ambles through the grass, then the sparrows swoop in and mince the crumbs. A tomato plant is taking shape growing, as is a good-rooted snap pea plant. Gotta dig out the damn slender bamboo shoots sneaking into the garden patch, already got a stalk-thick forest. Might be edible for koalas, which I heard eat bamboo—or is that eucalyptus leaves? Really can't say—never met a koala.

Not much happening in this part of the world, waiting out the plague, crunching the occasional spider, water bug, or large ant seeking food or worse, a home. No cockroaches. Left those critters behind long ago in that city high-rise apartment on Rhode Island Avenue, Northwest. That's a memory: neighbors battled roaches but never won; residents used duct tape in the kitchen, even arsenic. Roaches kept coming, in cabinets of jam and sugar and drawers of silverware. Not in closets. Upon coming home, turning on a light, got shivers from skippering on spindly legs. Never got used to roaches. Flies ain't so bad, living in the country. Now that I think about the differences.

Aches are not the worst, neither is forgetting. My hair hasn't changed to gray but thinner, scalp showing. Once thought of going skin-headed for a summer, not winter. No pain in that body part unless one considers memory. Can't recall forgetting anyway, 'cause how could one forget if one didn't know in the first place? Not remembering is a problem if the gas or flame is left on, not so much with electrical gadgets. Once forgot a metal pot heating water for tea for two, left it on that stove coil. Boy, a lot of scouring and erasing dark crud. Nope, learned one can't relax watching TV sitcoms either while reheating leftovers. Smells awful, for hours.

Oldies blare from the tired Magnavox radio nowadays. They're not oldies to those who heard the songs when they were top tens back then; somehow, one never forgets the words. Might carry a title name, like Sheri Bay-Bee or a line like *first time ever I saw your face*. A melody forms images of nights, crazy moments at the Bon Ton, and the lyrics prompt singing, even now; the next is a Motown spinning an urban beat—thumb snaps against index finger, and legs wobble to rhythm. Never thought those were the good old days. Faces appear in the mind, friends gone from venues dark, saucy, and loud: *hey, who's buying?* On comes a sad love song now: *If I see you walking down the street, walk on by.* Music keeps the sanity, kinda frames a good side of history—stories, laughs, and loves. Alone's not half-bad but can't play two-handed scrabble. Miss hearing her triumphant voice calling out, *fifty points, gotcha*—for one row of letters. There's depth to silence remembering vitality and thick hair—not burnt roaches.

Feeling sleepy after a bite of lunch calls for a nap, digestion kicks in. Kill off an hour or so prone; anyway, heat outside has piled up. Noise and bustle come through an open window: big trucks and a horde of roaches wearing construction site outfits. *What the—?* almost comes out. Go outside and look for a supervisor, stepping past chirping birds, two alley cats. Blurt out, *who's in charge?* and, *hey, watch those tomato stems and snap pea vines with that heavy equipment. Who's the boss? Bob, over there talking to that woman.* Call out, *hey, Bob.* He doesn't turn his head from flirting. Folks wandering like ants streaming the alley. Can't get close, wait. *Hey, Bob, what ya doin'? Oh, fixing a water line, sir, and digging a hole. Sir?* Not now.

I ain't gone, not yet. Back inside and close windows, block out noise, the world, and all haphazard changes. Turn off the radio and wait for darkness, sitting there. No TV news, set the radio on alarm. Fill up on Chianti red wine over and over. Anger rises in the glass. Moths come flitting silently about, and one fat fly buzzing. No sounds: birds gone by darkness. No meow-clawing—the cat's retired home. In the midst, ghosts of old faces pass and nod their heads in recognition. Try recalling names; oh yeah, what's-his-name, but no one's listening. Not any aches except a pain riding under the left arm. A faintness and stumble over the small table to the wooden floor. Ceiling fan on low spin, a gentle breeze. Heart's fine—I'm still here. Feel that rustling of vigor inside as the radio alarm pops on, blaring an old song, *Ain't no mountain high enough.*

Hell, no, wine talking now—not yet. Midst of all, wonder where word *pandemic* came from anyway? Read about Spanish flu back in 1918; learned that poet fella Robert Frost caught the flu, not once but twice, and survived; and who's the other writer, Dos Pasos? Said he couldn't write in a quarantine. Numbed fingers aren't as agile wrestling technology; words misspelled, hey, that's not correct. Stay in touch with oldster friends, also alone and locked down. They'd seen better days, back when pain meant more than heartache. That somber fella, what's his name—Cohen, Leonard?—he got the words right—said an ache in places I used to play. These text messages aren't human. Want to write more than sentiment, like, *hope you're doing okay*, and only say, *I'm fine too—here alone, eating a salad of tomatoes and snap peas.*

No, not yet. Still boil water in that burnt pot, enough for two cups of Chamomile tea after giving up coffee brew. Only sad thing is watching one teacup grow cold. Still feed birds dry white bread and chase the fighting cats and water the garden patch. Talk to neighbors, 'cause have-to. Wait on garbage collection and hope for mail. Garden not as green without her hands in the soil; if she needed help—she'd call out. Not a room in the house her voice doesn't still echo, as if she were arranging stuff, words humming in mind when she'd ask, *are you goin' help out today?* No urge to complete to-do things

now. Didn't think there might be agony in being not gone—
and didn't prepare for living alone in the midst.

A poetic-fiction tribute to families who survived a loss in the midst.

George Lies *a former journalist and author of many short stories:*
Rafaello's Night (2016):
http://www.heartwoodlitmag.com/georgemlies/
Trailer Dogs Barking (2008):
http://www.hamiltonstone.org/hsr16stories.html#trailerdog sbarking
Gone in Eight Seconds (2016):
https://shortfictionbreak.com/gone-in-eight-seconds/.

A past president of WVW, Inc., he started Morgantown Writers Group (1994).

Surviving Lockdown in Italy

George Lies – Morgantown, West Virginia, USA

Photo by George Lies

ITALY ON LOCKDOWN — Resilient Italians adjusted their lifestyles. Cleaning supplies (left) in hand, they relished the memories of Duomo di Milano (lower right), a card game called *Briscola*, and sipped espresso to rise. They drank toasts of wine with pasta dinners and displayed colorful flowers for love of life.

Social Isolation Solitude

Eldon Winston – Martinsburg, West Virginia, USA

Alone at home with my cellphone,
    In touch but out of reach.
Mask in hand I go forth
    this week's food to buy.

Shopping up and down the aisles
    I follow the arrows
    front to back and back to front.
Finally with a cart full of groceries
    I stand in line six feet behind
    the next in line.

Then home again, unload the groceries.
Alone I put things away in an empty house.
I read my paper and think
    the world is upside down.
We are isolated yet still rely on others.

The heat pump dies with the thermometer at 93.
I wait four days in a baking oven.
Oh! For a basement to cool me down.

A week passes and I take my mask in hand
    to get my week's food and
    visit the Hardware store.
Almost like old times but still alone.
No Party!

Eldon Winston says: *Writing for fun has been one of my hobbies for decades. When I was younger, I'd practice the craft after I got home from work or school, but now I'm just trying to express my views to the world. Not too bad for an Industrial Psychologist.*

Thank You

Crystal Brennan-Yeo and Alexa Yeo (10 years old) – Goderich, Ontario, Canada

An Acrylic Painting: Thank You

My daughter wanted to thank frontline workers. She composed a song on the harp and enlisted help from over 50 children in dedication. Together we painted this picture for donation to the local hospital in honour of all those sacrificing their safety and lives to hold up our world.

Crystal Brennan-Yeo is a secondary school arts teacher, and her daughter Alexa is 10 years old. Both enjoy playing the harp and spending time painting and performing together.

They created this piece of artwork to say 'Thank You' to all the frontline and essential workers risking their lives during this pandemic.

In the Midst of Darkness, Is There any Hope?

Zakia Salod – Durban, KwaZulu-Natal, South Africa

The year is 2020 and the COVID-19 pandemic sweeps the globe. With the number of infections and deaths rising, there is darkness everywhere . . . is there any hope?

"Lockdown!" "Use your mask!" "Social distance!" "Sanitize!" is the new norm. All of this because there is no COVID-19 vaccine (or drug) of any form.

Schools, universities, businesses, travels, events are closed and cancelled. Teach, study, work, and opt for virtual events; technology seems to be the viable solution instead.

Retrenchment and poverty are other pandemics happening. Disorder, confusion, disruption is the order of the day—it is very frightening.

Scientists and medical researchers are racing to find a COVID-19 vaccine. It is a race against time of the extreme.

We have no protection against COVID-19. We have no immunity. Indeed, we are all at risk, as humanity.

Darkness upon darkness . . . is there any hope in sight?
Wait for a COVID-19 vaccine, Pray and Trust The Almighty—
as with everything, there will most definitely be light.

*Thirty-year-old **Zakia Salod** lives in Durban, South Africa. He's a software developer, medical informatics scientist, data scientist, researcher, author, artist, and philanthropist. His role model is Prophet Muhammad (Peace Be Upon Him). He says, "I strive to do everything to please The Almighty Allah."*

There Is Hope

Zakia Salod – Durban, KwaZulu-Natal, South Africa

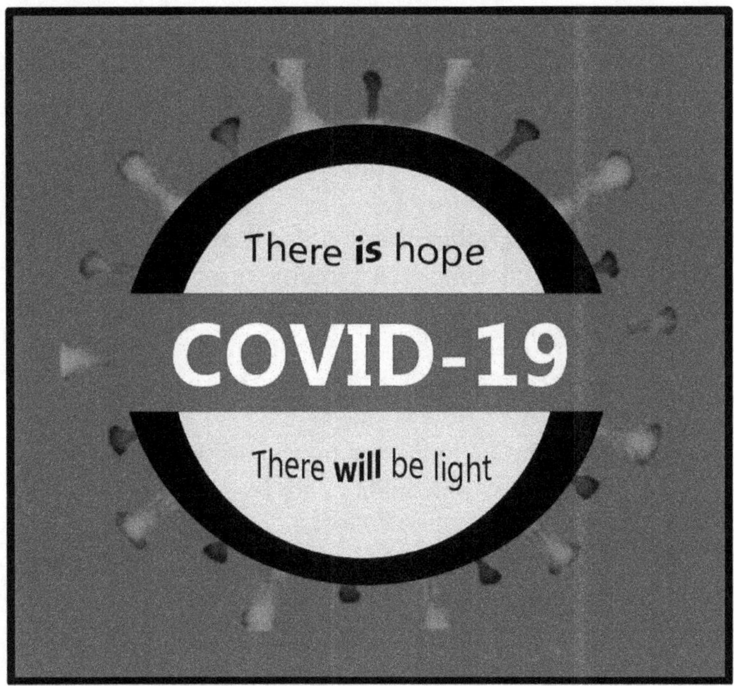

This artwork depicts the Severe Acute Respiratory Syndrome Coronavirus 2 (SARS-CoV-2) which causes the current and ongoing global Coronavirus Disease 2019 (COVID-19) pandemic. The black symbolizes the darkness that prevails in the world because of this virus. The yellow epitomizes hope and light in the midst of this darkness.

*Thirty-year-old **Zakia Salod** lives in Durban, South Africa. His bio appears on the previous page.*

PPE

David B. Prather – Parkersburg, West Virginia, USA

The face you see is   not mine,
by which I mean there is nothing left

of the youth I remember.
What's left is but a covering,

a representation of something I never thought
I would become. Veil, disguise, masquerade.

If only I could   stop time
by obscuring my face. The world is too

quiet, and there are too many mirrors
in this house. I wouldn't dare face you

without concealing my worst features.
Thin lips, long nose, the divot that runs

between them. I will thin my voice with cloth
so you can't detect my last cup of coffee,

my meaning cloaked. I'm so used to thinking
with my chin on my fist,   feeling

bare knuckles against square jaw.
Please, don't look at me. Keep a safe distance

between us. I will never show you the damage
done. I am far too old   for that.

David B. Prather *is the author of* We Were Birds. *He studied writing at Warren Wilson College and acting at the National Shakespeare Conservatory. His work has appeared in several journals, including* Prairie Schooner, Colorado Review, Poet Lore, The American Journal of Poetry, *and others. He lives in Parkersburg, West Virginia.*

Thrust Into Narnia by COVID-19

Jennifer Johnston Crow – Belpre, Ohio, USA

I was chatting with my friend Heather the other day, something we do almost every week. I'm incredibly grateful the pandemic has no impact on our conversations—she lives in South Africa and I in the United States, and we've never met face-to-face in the physical world. Our go-to is Zoom. It's a bright spot for me, where isolation is a non-issue.

Despite having only a virtual connection, we have a lot in common. Heather piques my intellectual curiosity, challenges my thinking on many levels, and we connect with our shared roles as coaches. I consider her as close a friend as those I see regularly (or used to, anyway).

Though the pandemic hasn't impacted our relationship, it's made for some interesting conversations since COVID-19 arrived. South Africa is under a strict lockdown right now, and, while we are certainly asked to shelter in place here, we are not as restricted as they. We got to talking about when this will all end and normalize (unanswerable, of course, not to mention that we will likely birth a whole new normal) and segued into a conversation about C. S. Lewis, author of many things but beloved for his seven-book children's series, *The Chronicles of Narnia.*

And that's when I just stopped mid-sentence. "It's always winter," I muttered as my thoughts started patterning. "It's as if we've walked through a wardrobe somewhere and entered a world where it's always winter and never Christmas."

As Lucy, Peter, Susan, and Edmund Pevensie did in Lewis's *The Lion, The Witch, and The Wardrobe*, we've stumbled our way into a world locked in winter—a world held in stasis by the White Witch (let's just call it Corona), who has forged a glisteningly cold, lonely, and fairly inhospitable place that's just waiting, pining for normalcy to return. Our entire world, like Narnia, is paused and isolated—literally as well as figuratively—in lockdown, sheltering in place.

Always winter and never Christmas. Can you even imagine? Can you feel the anticipation, the desire to again have Christmas and spring? Scouring the world for any little sign that it's coming, but especially a sign with the date, time, and, yes, year, please, when life will be normal again? Maybe even a clearer picture of what that new normal will look like?

Of course, you can! We are there right now: like those Narnians, we are in varying stages of denial, fear, boredom, worry, loss, grief—you name it.

Just the other day, my friend Brenda nearly broke my heart. That irrepressibly happy, cheerful woman popped onto my SKYPE screen with such an atypically sad countenance and demeanor that I was alarmed. It was obvious that the uncertainty had ensnared her thinking and taken her to a place of despair in that moment. She's certainly not alone; it's done that for all of us at one time or another. And, like most of us, Brenda was fine the following day. But it's an unfortunate testament to the power of the wintry world we inhabit across the globe.

In Narnia, it was the White Witch who levied the curse and Aslan the Lion who broke it. For the world today, it's the Coronavirus that levies the curse and a yet-to-be-invented vaccine that will break it.

Or perhaps, more accurately, it's the faith that we will be able to develop that vaccine quickly, find potential treatments in the interim, and follow guidance from those who can advise us intelligently on masks, physical distancing, and just plain common sense. God helps those who help themselves.

I imagine the rejoicing at each step will be amazing! The power of Corona will begin to fade with each new sign of thawing until the final moment when a safe and effective vaccine arrives, and our winter—like Narnia's winter—finally brings Christmas and spring. And summer and fall. Normalcy, whatever that looks like.

But for now, I think we're all a little bit lost in a Narnia of global proportions. For a world that likes control, it's a hard place in which to sit. We are lost in the not-knowingness of when it will end, of when we can resume our lives-before-Corona. We are lost in the dangers of the 24/7 nearly inescapable information overload. We are lost in our fears and obsessions. And we are lost in the insecurity of our future.

Ah, but even in Narnia under winter's grasp, the citizens—the fauns, the beavers, the deer, the badgers, and all the others—maintained hope, continued to put one foot in front of the other doing the next right thing, adapted to the wintry environment, and loved, cherished, supported, and helped one another through it all.

Like those Narnians who persevered and thrived despite those harsh circumstances, we can, too. We can choose to limit the barrage of information. We can protect and nurture others in ways that fit with our skills and abilities. We can practice leaning into uncertainty and learn from that experience in positive ways. We can, like the Narnians of Lewis's imagination, be resourceful, contented, happy, effective, and positive.

Lewis may as well have been writing in 2020 when he wrote these words in his book: "Why, it is she that has got all Narnia under her thumb . . . It's she that makes it always winter. Always winter and never Christmas; think of that!"

Yes, think of that for a moment. Feel the tension of what Dr. Steven Garber of the Washington Institute for Faith, Vocation, and Culture called "the tension of the now-but-not-yet of history and hope." Granted, it feels overwhelmingly weighted on the side of "not yet" instead of "now." But there's learning to be found there. There's living and innovating, gratitude and purpose, and maybe, just maybe, there's also happiness and serenity to be found in that tension. What we nurture there will surely move us unerringly through this lingering winter into Christmas, and far, far beyond.

I believe it, just as much as I believe in Narnia. (And I believe in Narnia.)

Jennifer Johnston Crow *is a personal, relationship, and group coach who's passionate about gratitude and writing. She's a West Virginian by birth and relatively recently moved two miles across the river into Ohio, but she tells everyone she's a "West Virginian currently living in Ohio." She blogs semi-regularly at jcrowcoaching.com.*

Wild Words

Anke Hodenpijl – Bakersfield, California, USA

be warned
this street will fill again
with kids riding bikes
Muslims walking their constitutional
weight watchers jogging
homeless collecting cans
teenagers ear buds in, oblivious to it all
dogs pulling on leads
the smell of family barbecues
basketballs bouncing
motorcycles roaring
pickle ball and preschoolers at the park

boomers around the propane campfire
lounge lizards on the driveway sipping ice-cold beer
will retell the Pandemic Folklore
how the patio was built in record time
how we binged on Netflix
how kids missed their playmates and school
how we learned to eat dinner at the table, became family
    again
how neighbors waved and greeted us when we walked the
    streets
how we dodged the bullet. We, the quarantine heroes.

we will leave this street
on our way to a place
not nearly as important
you will hear wild words:
I love you
Let me help you
Thank you

be ready
it will happen

Anke Hodenpijl's work has appeared in Writing Sound *(2019),* Reaching for the Sky *(2018),* Writing Flora, Writing Fauna *(2018), and others. Her love of poetry started as an easy way to learn the English language, soon morphing into a love for words masquerading as dance through poetry.*

For Our Grandchildren

Sherry Taylor Belisle – Woodstock, Vermont, USA

May 2020

I asked my father to write his memoir some years ago. He grew up in Southern Illinois, was a navigator in World War II, and, as an engineer, built the device that kept the Apollo rocket in orbit. He answered, yes, but on the condition that I would write my own stories. "The world is changing exponentially faster in your time than it was in mine," he said.

I'm aware that the present does become the past, and so, for my grandchildren and their own branches of the family tree, here is one chapter that merits involvement.

Like the Spanish Flu of 1918-1919, the COVID-19 flu of 2020 is wiping out millions throughout world. Although we have more scientific evidence for how to prevent getting disease than a hundred years ago, unfortunately, thousands in our country have already died. To try to prevent the illness from spreading, we are told to wash our hands frequently, stay at home, not mingle with anyone outside of our home, stay at a distance of six feet, and wear a mask when not home.

The results are empty streets and closed doors. As we pass by the library and the small downtown area, we feel as if we are in some other world; the old one has left and it will be a long time before it returns to safety. I see it as "mythical." Because our village is so small, we usually run into friends and acquaintances on the street when we're running errands. Even a familiar face of someone we don't know merits a smile. Now it's a rare occurrence.

If we need a prescription, we call ahead with our credit card number, stand six feet from the door, and reach to receive it from a clerk, both of us in masks. The grocery store has directional arrows in the aisles and only a certain number may enter at a time. Clerks are behind plastic walls and also wear masks. If we want restaurant dishes, we call ahead and take out. Although the food may be just as delicious, it's not the same as dining in a room with others.

No dental appointments, no elective surgery. No haircuts.

There is no hugging or even touching. I've literally "lost touch." I've always had an intent to touch senior citizens, especially those living alone, because I know that touch is important to human intimacy and, especially, to calmness.

No meeting together for any reason. That means no rites of passage for graduates like our grandson Wyatt from Martha's Vineyard High School and Dunovan from the University of Massachusetts at Amherst. No proms. No wedding ceremonies in a church or even outdoors with others unless the gathering is small. Even worse, no one can hold a loved one's hand while he or she dies. Memorial services are all "to be held at a later date."

There are so many losses of occupations. Stores and colleges shut down permanently, like MacMurray, where Bob and I met.

Our hair grows to longer lengths, creating styles of which we are not fond!

Although I have enough activities to keep me from feeling depressed as others are saying they are, I wonder if people feel as if they've lost their life's purpose. Socializing in person is considerably different than talking on the phone or even through an internet application.

Working not only supports people, but it also gives their lives meaning. Often, those who have worked all their lives are at a loss when they retire. This is forced retirement for many when it's not their choice. The weekly paycheck stops, and they must ask for food and fuel assistance.

Now there is nothing to put a calendar in our heads. Weekdays are the same as weekends, except for a sermon recorded remotely, but even that can be listened to later in the week. For years, my writing group has met in our home on Tuesday afternoons. Our prompt is set on Mondays or Tuesdays now, and we can write whenever we want.

Feedback from others is via email. It's different than seeing my friends smile as they support my written words.

I've never been an avid shopper, but now we must have something particular in mind when we want an item locally. No more browsing for a card, a gift or an article of clothing. No perusing the library shelves for a book or opening the cover to have a glimpse of what it's about. Taking to an iPad for reading would not have been my choice.

Children and teachers are struggling to work through their computers only. The students miss the socialization of being at school, and working with a parent is not at all like working with their teacher.

I make a point of dressing up each day, although I wouldn't have to. One could be in pajamas all day, even those who work from home.

Having said all this, there are positive points to the experience too. I've made face masks for the hospitals and anyone else who needs one. I've cleaned out things in the basement (at the bottom of my to-do list) and discovered treasures—pictures and mementos that tie me to earlier times. I found my Grandmother Maud Taylor's hundred-year-old, handmade, very well worn cotton quilt. I cut it into ten pieces and have made a pillow for each granddaughter and four samples in frames for the grandsons.

Upset about having to use plastic bags at the grocers instead of my own canvas ones, I've crocheted the plastic ones into a bag that will be good for produce at the Market on the Green this summer.

The era engenders creativity; many have been posting videos of songs about the virus and its effects that make us laugh. Choirs and orchestras meet virtually by Zoom to entertain. Museums open their doors online so we may visit for free. Virtual concerts are held for the benefit of those affected by the virus.

I've had time to convert videos to digital and have enjoyed watching our family grow up again. I've played piano more. I've sent cards that I've painted.

We play online games with Darren and his family, and our entire immediate family of seventeen chat weekly on Zoom. Before, it's always been family to family: T calls Darren or Darren calls Molly. Now we're all together, which is more fun.

Even more importantly, the earth is so much clearer of pollution. Nature ignores the virus, blessing us with spring blooms that warm our hearts and make us smile. I'm grateful this virus didn't make itself known at the cold of winter, especially Christmastime. That would be worse. We'll just have to see about this holiday season.

Before the virus, there were mass shootings way too regularly—in schools, churches, synagogues, theaters, and concerts. At least we have a reprieve from those terrible events.

Things are certainly easier here in Vermont, away from a city with so many close contacts, and it's clear that we are observing the rules well, because the virus count is relatively low. It will take a long time for us to recover enough to trust, to feel safe again. In the meantime, I pray for those who have lost those they love. One phrase that is oft repeated is "We're in this together." And together, we'll recover.

Sherry Taylor Belisle is a 50-year resident of Woodstock, Vermont, and moved there from Illinois. She's in a writers group and also enjoys penning memories for her family tree.

Who Knew?

Sandy Lynn Helm Moffett – Bakersfield, California, USA

Who knew that you could have too much quiet?

Who knew that you could tire of having too much time to read, fidget with puzzles, and rearrange closets and drawers?

Who knew that a Marco Polo or FaceTime chat with family would be the highlight of your day?

Who knew that you would see pulling weeds as an adventure?

Who knew it wouldn't matter if you didn't vacuum or make the bed or leave a dish in the sink overnight, because no one would be coming to your house?

Who knew that an act of kindness—a flower left on your doorstep or a teenager offering to return your cart—would bring a swell to your heart and unstoppable tears to your eyes?

Who knew that the meaning of a word could change?

"Normal."

Who knew?

I didn't.

Did you?

Sandy Lynn Helm Moffett *was born in Bakersfield, CA, and returned to her hometown in 1985. She has been married to Greg for 39 years, and they have four children and 12 grandchildren.*

Sandy is a poet and lyricist, and has been published in Chicken Soup for the Soul, Cup of Comfort, *and numerous other works.*

Photo by Sandy Moffett

The gift of a flower—even this masterpiece of creation—has been touched by COVID. The petals fall like our spirits. The soil dries up like our dreams. But wait—there is a new bud. A new day, a new hope, a new promise. We have survived, and we'll be okay.

COVID-19 Rant

Wilma Stanley Acree – Vienna, West Virginia, USA

Reporters call me old, aged, senior,
like I'm a piece of roadside rubbish . . .
Cover your mouth and nose with a mask;
it won't help you, just protect others.

I am here to tell you guys
there ain't no mask that'll protect you—
or this virus—from old age.
Age is as sneaky as any virus.

And there ain't no use to talk
about going back to normal.
We ain't ever goin' back
to Corona being just a beer.

Wilma Stanley Acree *lives with a cat and a dog in Vienna, West Virginia, USA. Her poems have appeared in numerous literary journals and anthologies. She is an active member and past president of West Virginia Writers, Inc.*

COVID-19 Temple

Robert Fleming – Lewes, Delaware, USA

a minion is 1 2 many
10 men meeting, must not
the mezuza door is unkissed
matches light the wick wax
the torah is unread
hold hands around the temple,
6' hands apart
doven the children of Abraham
prayers for a prophet
deliver the messiah 2 re-open the temple

Robert Fleming *lives in Lewes, DE. He is a member of the Rehoboth Beach & Eastern Shore Writer's Guild. In 2019, he was nominated for a Lambda Literary Award as a contributor to the poetry anthology* Stonewall Legacy. *Upcoming Fall, 2020 publication of four poems* in Broadkill Review.

Hope: Light in the Storm

Owen Kirchner (11 years old) – Chatham, New Jersey, USA

Oil pastels on paper.

Owen Kirchner is an eleven-year-old who lives in New Jersey. His father commuted into New York City every day for work before the pandemic stay-at-home order. Owen drew this picture for his distance-learning art class—the assignment was to draw emotion. Owen said, "The lightning represents bursts of hope in the dark storm of the COVID–19 crisis. There is always light that's present, even in tough times."

The Gathering Gene

Evie Groch – El Cerrito, California

Now that normal has been evicted
it's up to us foragers
to step out into the fear to gather food
sustain the clan,
restore humanity and humility,
unite the citizenry, dispel the lies.

We speak softly with thoughtful words,
tread lightly against threats,
strip a tyrant of his armies,
plan a path toward a pandemic of trust.
We know what others still must learn:
Fires, tornadoes, tsunamis
cannot be bullied into submission.
Neither can viruses.

So let us put on our hardship boots,
lift our shields or hold our breath,
march out with compassion,
empathy and an outstretched arm
to show what caring, intelligent
leaders can do.
Lace 'em up!

Evie Groch has been in education all her life, but at a mature age, the love of travel and writing lured her over to the creative side where she has been publishing in every genre imaginable. Always up for a challenge, she writes on.

Little Red (fiction)

Karen H. Mays – Port Elizabeth, Eastern Province, South Africa

Back in 1897 when HG Wells wrote *War of the Worlds*, or in 1949 when George Orwell penned his now classic novel, *1984,* and even as recently as 2019, no one could have predicted the events of 2020. It reads like fiction—or science fiction. Nobody dreamed life as we knew it would soon be ripped to shreds as a tiny, quiet, deadly microorganism systematically worked its way through our communities.

When the year 2020 dawned, we welcomed the new decade with all the arrogance and hedonism of a race of "intelligent" beings, secure in the knowledge that we were the rulers of the earth. Little did we know it then, but life had other plans.

Shortly before, in Wuhan, China, a powerful warrior was born. Little Red, a strange little fellow. He didn't quite fit in anywhere. He didn't look like his mum or his dad. He didn't look like his brothers or sisters. In fact, he didn't look like anyone in his family. Little Red was an anomaly. But it was his difference that made him so unique and so special, and it was his uniqueness that gave him his strength and his power.

When his family teased him and his brothers and sisters laughed at him, Little Red kept quiet, because he had a secret. Every time they tormented him, he grew stronger. Every time they teased him, he became braver and tougher. Even though he looked tiny, Little Red was only tiny on the outside. On the inside, he was powerful, tenacious, courageous, and patient. He was smart—and a great teacher. Quietly and secretly, he hatched his plan. And in 2020, Little Red finally showed his hand—and he was named King and was crowned Corona-19. And in 2020, Corona-19 ruled the world.

As human beings, we are a complex species, surprisingly full of contradictions. We have the capacity to hate or to love in equal measure, and to create or destroy. Yet for a race of supposedly intelligent beings, the human race is sometimes frighteningly unintelligent. We think we are superior to the creatures of the oceans and the animals of the earth, and yet we shackle ourselves to a life of servitude and enslave ourselves to debt—not only as a means of survival, but often from greed. We tie ourselves to consumerism in the quest for more, bigger, better—and in so doing, we destroy the very home we call our own, this Blue-Green planet called Earth.

When Corona-19 became king, he was a cruel leader, reminding us of our human fragility. Our world was gripped in a global pandemic—a pandemic that caused pandemonium. It wrought havoc with our health and security, created anxiety and uncertainty. Devastated world economies, infected millions, and killed thousands. Unemployment soared. Schools closed. Conspiracy theories and confusion flourished. We were a world under siege. Not from armies of invaders, but victims of our own arrogance. COVID-19 was both respected and feared. And he came with a powerful message for humankind.

This beautiful planet we call Earth does not need us. It has survived billions of years without us and will survive billions of years after we are gone. The world does not need humanity. Humanity needs the world. Only humanity needs humanity. We need each other.

As a whole, humanity is just a speck in the Universe, and, as individuals, our impact is tiny and fleeting. And yet, each one of us has the capacity to make an enormous impact during our brief time on this planet.

If something so small and seemingly insignificant as Little Red can have such an astronomical impact on our world, what impact can humankind have? We have the capacity to do great things.

Corona-19 came here to teach us a lesson—to remind us of our true nature. His message is peace and love, connection and harmony. We are **Humanity**—Human Beings with the innate capacity for Love and Kindness, Caring and Generosity.

It is time to understand that no matter our race, gender, ethnicity, social status, culture, creed, or religion, we are all the same. We are born into this world to make our mark for a brief moment in time, and one day soon, we will leave this world. The question is, will we leave this world a better place than we found it? What will be our mark and our legacy? Individually—and united? The 21st century will forever be delineated "Pre-CV-19" and "Post-CV-19." The world cannot go back to the way it was before.

Now is the time for us to return to our roots, to a simpler way of living, to a humbler way of being. It is time to embrace our Humanity. It is time to step up and accept our true role as Human Beings—to revere all life and to respect all living things, no matter how great or small. It is time to understand we too are small and insignificant in the grand scheme of things. And yet, we have a significant part to play. Our contribution, no matter how tiny, can have a ripple effect to create huge momentum and change.

If one tiny micro-organism like Little Red can have the impact to change the world, just imagine the power of 7.8 billion magnificent Human Beings coming together to reinvent our world and create a new world. A world of love. A world of peace. A world of caring.

2020 is the dawning of a new age, a new era, a new world. A world infected with a natural virus known as Human Kindness. A virus that will spread around the earth and infect everyone it touches with peace, love, harmony, caring and connection. Because we are Human**kind**. We are Humanity. We are Kind. We are **The Human Race**. And we Love Our World.

Human Kindness - Corona-21

Karen H. Mays is a wife, mother, daughter, writer, and Design a Dream Life Coach living in Port Elizabeth, South Africa, with her husband Neil, her Mum, Jean, and her two dogs, Rosie and Buddy. She has two grown sons and their partners, who are her greatest pride and joy.

COVID-19: Fatal Pandemic: Voice of Hope

Tabani Mtwana – Mthatha, Eastern Cape, South Africa

The global outbreak—
A virus that has the world's livelihood at stake—
Touching, coughing, breathing, sneezing
Those simple human daily orthodox are not pandemic
pleasing.

Liaising with necessary precautionary measures—even
though the virus "faced" at "hand"—the answer lies in
"masked" and "sanitised."
Keep quarantined, dear human of the soil—outside is no
distinct victim immortalized,
Like no thunderstorm ever endured; globally we should keep
our patterns centralized.

Shun to compliance is a rise to mass demise,
As though resembling the domino effect (0 to 6 cases)
initially; falling after the other, graves praising pandemic.

Beyond the mask—breathe!
Above your faith—believe!
From current state; looking backwards is remote.
WHO global state, a potential cure derivative to freedom
shall promote.
Before asking who's WHO? World Health Organisation came
to rescue.

*Tabani Mtwana is a twenty-three year-old South African
pursuing a career in the Arts. He's a self-taught visual artist
with the end goal to create content that will reach out to the
world at large in the form of paintings, drawings, exhibitions,
dance school, poetry chapbooks, and novels/nonfiction
books.*

COVID-19: Fatal Pandemic: Voice of Hope

Tabani Mtwana – Mthatha, Eastern Cape, South Africa

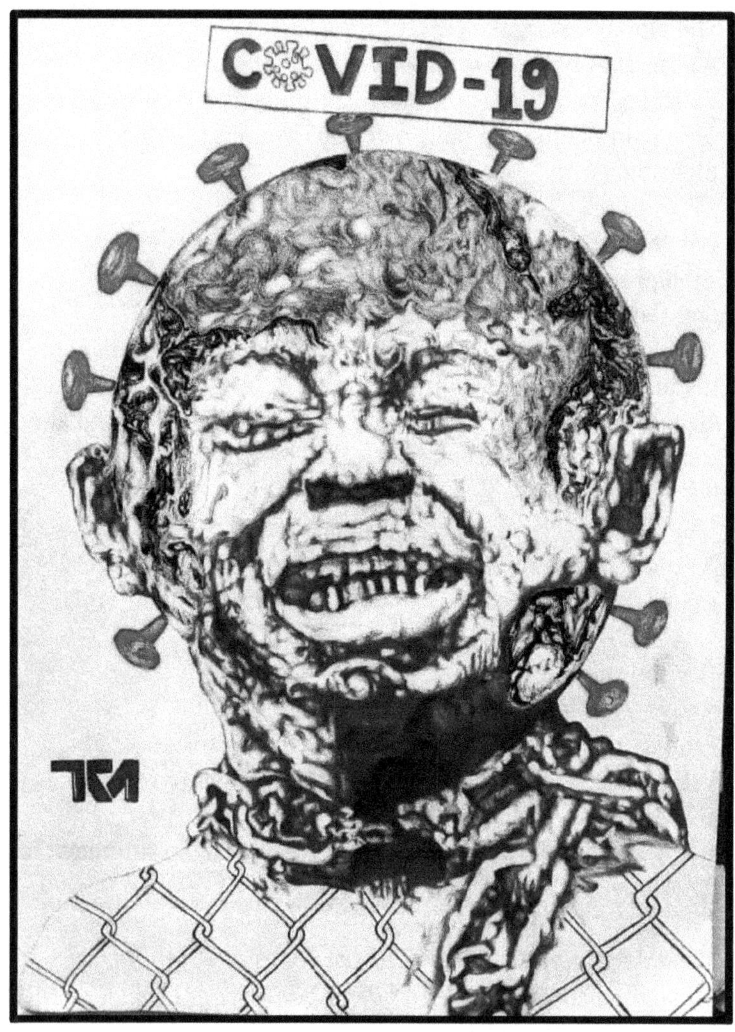

ABOUT THE ARTWORK:

The image reveals the face of an infant with tears—showing how the agony of a pandemic has reflected on innocent souls and how the newly adjusted norms of living have been enforced by authority and power—leaving the ordinary human feeling chained to the uncertainty of freedom in a world of many occurrences.

Tabani Mtwana is a twenty-three year-old South African pursuing a career in the Arts. He's a self-taught visual artist with the end goal to create content that will reach out to the world at large in the form of paintings, drawings, exhibitions, dance school, poetry chapbooks, and novels/nonfiction books.

2020 Vision

Lana Hunneyball– West Sussex, United Kingdom

Look up, it's lock down
The Boot is on our necks
COVID operations echo deafening peals
into the ripples of our fear
yours
smallness never collides conveniently with History.
It's never a good time to wake up
just as you're dying.

Wake up!
Democracy is By the people
for the people
By the people
For the people
Wake up
If you're having a good time
is someone paying the price?
Follow the money—where are the strings?
Is someone counting the seconds
like he did
as his smallness collided?

Like an atom
we break

Lana Hunneyball is a South African living in the UK and works as a live-in caregiver. She is working on a novel and other projects. She lives by the Erich Fromm quote, "Life is giving birth to yourself," and works daily to trust the still small voice. Her first poetry collection Flotsam and Jetsam *will be published shortly.*

Inside My Writing Lair

Cookie Cranston – Johnston, Iowa, USA

I didn't see it coming. No one did. And it was charging at us full speed ahead. Barreling in like a runaway freight train loaded with explosive, scary, unknown players, some posing as co-protagonists in a poorly written elementary suspense-writing assignment. No rational brain could comprehend this. It was difficult, if not impossible, to fully fathom the immensity of a world health pandemic. Perhaps equally impossible was to classify the genre of such a narrative as this—Mystery? Horror? World history? Sci Fi? Fiction? I'm a writer, and when I write fiction, I make stuff up. But this! THIS! Irreverent imagination!

It WAS real, all right. Surreal is more accurate—the intense irrationality of a nightmare. For sure! The best way for me to deal with stress is to write about it, so I decided immediately to chronicle the events by keeping a journal. (Snippet excerpts from my journal will appear in italics).

It was on March 11, 2020, that a Corona Virus health pandemic was officially declared in the US. Panic and paranoia mount, and as reports surface, people begin to take it more seriously.

The back story: I had the good fortune to have just attended the Desert Nights, Rising Stars Writing Conference on the Arizona State University campus, returning home from Arizona the last week of February. A most fabulous experience. I floated back to the Midwest enthused, impressed, inspired, and affirmed with an energy to write like I had never written before. Walking on air! My feet barely touching the ground. I was euphoric after having met amazing, talented writers. I had found my tribe—including someone who was interested in potentially publishing some of my writing. I had no idea that my life in the following months would become such a bittersweet collision at the crossroads of a world health pandemic and a writer's sabbatical. A hiatus that most writers only dream of.

—groceries were flying off the shelves! People were stockpiling food and supplies. What are they afraid of? Can somebody please tell me why there is a shortage of toilet paper?

Suddenly, every single thing on my calendar was canceled or postponed. SHELTER IN PLACE! STAY HOME! SOCIAL DISTANCE! WASH YOUR HANDS! WEAR A MASK! Those precautions have been part of the everyday rhetoric. The month of April on my calendar became completely void of any plans or appointments. All that remained were haunting dark lines drawn through all that had been. Canceled. Life was eerily canceled. Aloneness reflected from that calendar and stared me in the face. It didn't take long for that reality to set in. Going forward, it would be just Bailey Bedford Moon (my aging Basset Hound companion) and ME—thank God for her.

—restaurants and bars were ordered to close today and everything else followed—schools, churches, salons, malls, festivals, proms, graduations, sporting events, theaters, plus new set limits of 10 people at weddings and funerals, etc.

Clearly everything but essential services was affected. Businesses closed. Some people worked from home, countless others lost their jobs. Millions filed for unemployment. It was utter social and economic chaos.

—a much anticipated socially-distanced visit from daughter.
—seventy million people were ordered to stay home. A slammed economy was in free-fall. Can't stop THAT freight train on a dime, let alone reverse it. More chaos.

Being somewhat familiar with adversity in my life, I knew I must quickly find a way to survive. Without completely understanding the immense scope of what was happening, I convinced myself I was not totally alone—I did have B, and I did, of course, have ME. I was alone, but I didn't have to be lonely. I was isolated, but I didn't have to sit idly by and let the world self-destruct around me. Landslides of information ripped through the media. I didn't really know what to believe. Truth? Lies? Stories? Projections? Speculation? Everything seemed to be a moving target, and the result was dizzying.

—Meme from Facebook: "About three weeks from now we will find out what everybody's REAL hair color is." And what about toilet paper? What is the obsession with toilet paper? My sense is I'm too busy getting organized to be alone.

My favorite pastimes are reading and writing. There would be ample time for both. But this didn't read like any story or any book I had ever read—turn the page and the rules had changed and the players were different. Conflicting narratives added to the confusion and unrest. All at once it was beware of people—friends, family, and neighbors. This new enemy is potentially all of those people in my closest circles, in my safest places—all whom I love and trust. The COVID-19 enemy is elusive. Every one, every thing, every place is now the potential host of the potential enemy, where shared spaces and human contact are the threat. I liken the unfathomable situation to Improv Theater—don't try to plan, just try to react. Punt! Make it up as you go.

A number of years ago, I wrote two children's concept picture books—*Sounds of Fall* and *Sounds of Winter*, treasures of interactive seasonal sensory impressions, intended to introduce children to a deeper understanding of our interconnectedness with the natural world. I came home from Arizona with a fire in my belly to finish writing the other two seasons. Little did I know that my writing would take on such energy and focus to fill such huge gaps during my sequestered time.

—Shakespeare wrote King Lear, Macbeth, *and* Antony and Cleopatra *while in quarantine during the Black Plague in 1606. Writers, get writing!*

I had a big goal and all the time in the world to give it. A perfect storm, and with so many people suffering, I felt a great responsibility to use the time wisely. I was compelled to stay home and stay safe and determined to emerge from my forced cocoon status with something tangible. My writing has always been healing and liberating, and it would become even more so this time. I want my little books to become the beautiful butterflies released from that cocoon that flutter into the hands of children.

The unsettling days turned into weeks, and the weeks slowly drifted into months. Life would never be the same. There were tears at times, but no one to dry them except my sensitive canine. Introspection ran deep with no distractions. I found myself actually grieving over losses of normalcy, human connection, financial security, economic collapse, and physical and emotional suffering by so many. The greatest tragedy for me has been such limited time with family and loved ones and the realization of how fragile life has become. But all the while, my writing continued with intensity, and as time went on I began to recognize and heal from many of my own hurts and wounds.

I have spent the majority of my time these last four months writing—hours and hours and hours of writing. A.M./P.M., daylight/dark, rain/shine—it didn't matter. Time stood still and was eerily quiet at times, uninterrupted by anyone. By anything. I have completed the four children's manuscripts and more. I'm a writer on a roll, and I am oddly thankful for this unexpected oasis to write.

I told my daughter that if I contracted this virus or if something else wacky or unexpected happened to me during this distorted time in our lives, to not ever think of me living in my aloneness, but to always think of me rambling happily about in my own little world. Talking and listening to my writer's voice and reading my work aloud to B, totally being okay to just be me. Not thinking about the what-ifs and worries of tomorrows, being better for having learned to live in the moment and closer to the center of me. Thinking of the next word, dreaming of the next sentence, imagining the next story.

—Cases of COVID-19 have increased in many states in the past week. Six states report more than a 50% jump in positive cases . . . normalcy may not return until next year following the spikes. Grim projection that there may be more than 200,000 deaths by October 1. Alarming! And the beat goes on.

I hope I can look back at this someday and vividly recall the poignant rare footage of life that unfolded. Unraveled. And I have unapologetically decided to live it in the present, immersing myself in writing my own headlines. I can't depend on the world or anyone in it to do that for me. In my seclusion I am surviving and living the life of an empowered writer. Safe. Deep inside my writing lair.

Cookie Cranston *is a retired (after 32 years) high school library employee who brushed up against the books of many writers and illustrators and vowed that when she retired, she too would write. When she's not reading, writing, or gardening, she's spoiling her canine companion, Bailey.*

COVID-19 Social Distance

Robert Fleming – Lewes, Delaware, USA

& now they're none,
humans, 6' together,
earth overseer repealed my bill of rights,
2 congregate with 10 humans -
soul with my > 10,000 germs -
my house wall divides me
50' from another human –
if only i had a jackhammer 2 break thru
2 my neighbor,
nah, better,
if only i was a leopard –
id still be sole,
but wear a black skin or spots,
& show my saw teeth,
with a big cat hiss!
not i, cat 2 b,
4 im a hu-man
&, damn, i can't transmute my 2 legged
backbone into 4 legged leopard;
as consolation, i connect 2 the www
with rollbar fingertips,
& phone screen fingertips,
& after, i can no longer bare
2 view my > 500 videos,
ill self-evict, me,
the last man in my house
& launch my earth pod
& eject into?

Robert Fleming *lives in Lewes, DE, and is a member of the Rehoboth Beach & Eastern Shore Writer's Guild. In 2019, he was nominated for a Lambda Literary Award as a contributor to the poetry anthology* Stonewall Legacy. *Upcoming Fall, 2020, publication of four poems* in Broadkill Review.

Learn Social Distancing from your Cat

Sonya Gonzalez – San Antonio, Texas, USA

Feeling confined, I found myself staring eye-to-eye with my cat, who was stretched out on a table a few feet away. It dawned on me that I could learn the skill of social distancing from him—a master at it! A bowl of treats in hand for his effortless training. The painting is 12" x 12" acrylic on paper mounted on wood.

*Playing the violin at a young age led **Sonya Gonzalez** to painting later in life. Her art is also influenced by the Hispanic culture and nature; and has been featured on the covers of several magazines. She has exhibited locally and nationally and has written and illustrated several books.*

The 120 Species of Wuhan Market

JoAnn Lord Koff – Manassas, Virginia, USA

Unconscionably, a bushmeat virus
Is borne, in code, a deadly concoction, Shot into lungs,
squeezing oxygen out.

Instantaneously, we fall prey.
The old die younger than they should;
A lesson Wuhan animals learnt firsthand.

In 2020, COVID-19 became the only Craze to flourish
worldwide;
It consumed in rapidity.

Earth as ill as those who live upon it; Humans had forgotten
how to live as one, A cruel moral lesson revisited now.

Closed in, away from family; Separated, without food;
No work—economies falter.

Wild boars, spotted deer, foxes Penetrate cities; we hide in
homes, Wear masks, as the virus multiplies.

We can't hold hands, or kiss, Or communicate without risk;
Caged in a conundrum we created.

Life requires value; be it animal, a tree, a human, or a planet;
Without value, nothing flourishes
Mankind, the 121st victim of Wuhan Market.

JoAnn Lord Koff had a gallery show at the Center for the Arts/ ARTFactory in Manassas, Virginia, entitled "Camera Eyes: On Poetry" based on her poetry and photography book, Sand, Pebbles, Fossils, and Rocks, *which was nominated for the Library of Virginia's Literary Award for Poetry in 2019.*

Corona II, 2020

Alan Grobler – Port Elizabeth, Eastern Cape, South Africa

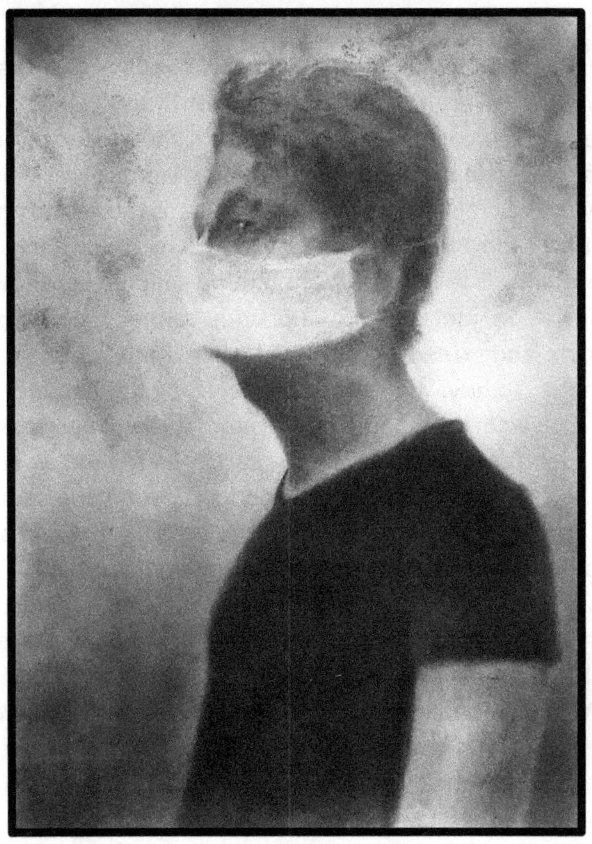

'Corona II, 2020': charcoal & mixed powder pigment 610mm x 470mm on Fabriano

Alan Grobler *of South Africa works mainly in the medium of woodcut and linocut printmaking, and large charcoal drawings. He studied graphic fine art and graduated with honours from the College for Advanced Technical Education. Retired from the Nelson Mandela Metropolitan Municipality as Library Promotions Coordinator, he is currently practising visual art fulltime.*

So Far Away

M. Lynne Squires – Scott Depot, West Virginia, USA

About 40 minutes on the freeway. That's not all that far, really. I've driven it a few times a month ever since he left home to go to college. We go to eat, to the grocery store, to the movies, and there for a while to the laundromat. The last trip was two weeks ago when I took him to the grocery store.

"But, Mom, I have plenty of food. I'm good, really." My son probably is telling the truth. But he acquiesces, knowing I will insist on stocking him up with canned goods, paper products, and some treats I know he likes but might not spend the money to buy. Who's to know how long this pandemic will last? A week in, and panic has ensued at the supermarkets. I want to ensure he has enough to carry him several weeks.

The store isn't terribly crowded, and everyone seems to be practicing social distancing. I have on a hoodie and spend a good part of the time with the front up over my mouth in lieu of a mask. The arms are pulled down over my hands, even though I have brought wipes with me to sanitize the buggy handle—and the child seat where I set my purse.

We make our way through the store, and I observe the things that are in good supply as well as what previously filled the empty shelves. There are ample amounts of canned fruits, but canned vegetables only have off-brand collard greens and some black-eyed peas huddled far in the back together. Soap is in abundance, but no hand sanitizer, nor any alcohol or aloe vera gel to make your own. Lots of flavored water, but nary a bottle of spring water—store brand or designer label.

At home, he unloads the haul while I wash his dishes. Not the first time, and likely not the last. We talk about trivial things. How his glass stovetop needs to be cleaned. His theory about his duplex neighbor possibly moving out. How the house smelt of hamster cage when he turned on the AC for the first time of the season.

We don't talk much about the elephant at first. The one standing between us as we dance around whether or not to be too close. To hug, to touch. We finally talk about news articles and press conferences. About numbers and countries and medical supplies. About supply and demand, and helplessness.

We never once let ourselves say we might not return to a recognizable normal for a long, long time. Both of us are still working. Me from home, and he goes into an office. I plead with him to sanitize his work area every single day. I worry he'll become lax. I did just wash a few days of his dishes, after all.

He assures me the staff cleans the spaces between shifts, and he does too because he doesn't trust them to be thorough. That makes me feel a bit better. But just a bit. He's in a call center doing surveys for the CDC and other health agencies. The irony of that isn't lost on me.

The day seems off, different from our other visits. The elephant has moved to the edge of the room, no longer between us, but still lurking. We never run out of things to say, usually. But today we just seem to be passing the time until I go. Back to my home, just 40 minutes away. But now separated by a chasm, a governor's order, an unseen menace. And an edge of fear sidling up beside us.

I've never felt so close to him. He's never seemed so far away.

M. Lynne Squires M. Lynne Squires is a Pushcart Prize nominated author of four books, including the award-winning Letters to My Son – Reflections of Urban Appalachia at Mid-Century. *A short story crafter, poet, and essayist, her work appears in numerous anthologies and journals. She was the recipient the 2020 Pearl Buck Writing for Social Change award.*

Wash Your Hands

Alma Pretorius – Gauteng, South Africa

Mask on,
Mask off,
Wash your hands.

Buy groceries,
Put groceries in fridge & pantry,
Wash your hands.

Celebrate your birthdays,
Eat some cake,
Wash your hands.

Celebrate your wedding anniversary,
Give your beloved a hug,
Wash your hands.

Zoom your family,
Zoom your friends,
Wash your hands.

Take out the rubbish bin,
Bring in the rubbish bin,
Wash your hands.

Say hello to neighbors,
Give apples to the birds,
Wash your hands.

Watch TV,
Eat dinner,
Wash your hands.

Do your exercises,
Walk around the block,
Wash your hands.

Get ready for bed,
Put lotion on your hands . . .
Do not wash your hands.

Alma Pretorius of South Africa says: I want to inspire people. I want to share my creativity and my passions. Life is amazing—Life is about choices—You can sit in a corner and be depressed—or you can stand on your toes and shout to the sky: "I'm alive! Let me be all I can be!"

Dentistry in the Pandemic (fiction)

John Deupree – Shepherdstown, West Virginia, USA

Will AI ease our concerns about dentistry if the pandemic continues?

I was a bit anxious about seeing the dentist. As my appointment approached, I strolled the room, finally sitting back down to pick through old magazines. At precisely 9:28, two minutes before the appointment time, the auto-taxi stopped in front of my house. A young woman stepped out, walked up the steps, and rang the doorbell.

I opened the door to the tall woman wearing tan slacks and a white blouse covered by a short surgical robe. Her fashionable mask complimented her red hair. Her pleasant, professional appearance immediately put me at ease. "Good morning. I am Dr. Edwards. How are you this morning?"

Despite her reassuring friendliness, I could only manage a curt, "Hello, Doctor," in response.

"A bit nervous, perhaps? Don't worry. This will all be quick and easy. We are constantly refining our procedures. Now, let's make sure we have the right diagnosis."

As she stretched out her right index finger, an air screen appeared. Running her finger down the screen, she stopped in the middle. "This should be it. You have a slight cavity in tooth twenty-two. Does that sound correct?"

I nodded.

"Perfect, and quite simple. In fact we have just finished testing a brand new process. Which chair is most comfortable for you?"

Feeling a bit more comfortable, I pointed to my favorite chair. "The Barcalounger is where I usually take naps."

The doctor turned to face the beige, faux-leather monstrosity in the corner of my living room.

"That will be perfect. Make yourself comfortable."

After sitting, I looked up at her and opened my mouth out of habit.

"Oh, no need to do that anymore. All of our procedures are external. Just relax. If you'd like, we can play a video. Our data says you are fond of Patagonia. I have one of hiking in the Andes. Would you like that?"

I nodded again, and she reached over and pulled off her left pinky. Looking around the room for a flat surface, she spotted the coffee table and set her finger on it. A full-color video appeared on the ceiling. I watched in awe as the glaciers, waterfalls, and wildlife floated by, and nearly forgot she was there.

"There, that should do it. Now, what I am going to do next is spread a laser heat shield on your right cheek. It won't hurt, although it may be slightly warm. "

She flipped open her left thumb, and a bright green gel oozed out over the edge. She carefully wiped it on my cheek. "I'm just going to make sure it's spread to the right thickness over the entire area. It will just take a minute."

After a pause, she continued, "Now, I'm simply going to use the laser to erase that cavity. Trust me, you won't feel anything."

With that, she reached up and touched her nose through her mask, turning it slightly to the right. Out of her left ear appeared a small flashlight-looking device that turned in its place, zeroing in on my cheek. "Hold still. This will only take a few seconds."

A red light flashed, and my cheek grew briefly warm. Then, just as suddenly, it was over.

"That's it. All done."

I was stunned. So simple and stress free. "Doc, I have to say that was just great. Thank you so much. What do I owe you?"

She reset the equipment in her head and index finger, returning to a normal human appearance. "Oh, no worries about that. It's all covered under Medicare-for-All. That program also funded the research for our procedures. And," she said, a slight smile, "we are expanding our services. Soon you'll be able to call us to examine your pets, do your taxes, and even shop for groceries, if you're unable to do that on your own. I'll leave you an air brochure."

She picked up her pinky finger projector, aimed it at the wall between the two portraits of my ancestors, and left the brochure hanging just an inch or two in front of them. The sunshine yellow paint on my wall showed through, giving it a sense of pleasant brightness. Then she screwed the finger back on and checked her watch. "We were thirty-seven seconds faster than anticipated, so the auto-taxi is still ninety seconds away. Would you mind if I use your bathroom while I wait? I have my own toilet paper and sanitizer."

John Deupree is an emerging writer based in Shepherdstown, West Virginia. His stories have appeared in several local anthologies, and he has just released his novella Bougainvillea. *A novel,* Fusion, *is in the works.*

Comes the Pestilence of 2020

Brenda Bunting – Oxon Hill, Maryland, USA

All the world we know is comprehended in a thin slice of
    gravity.
It must remain constant, as we must.
The air exchanges are a trusting push pull of exhilaration.
The symbiotic wonderment moves to ordinary in regularity.
But what if we suddenly cannot breathe. We are held down.
    Infected.

Hatred and transmission are dancing a fury ungodly.
All focus shifts to the impermanence.
The thin slices become harrowing instability.
They break apart into frail moments of paranoia.
We are dying many different ways.

Who shall help us when the healers die also?
Hearts of vulnerability shredded by the unrelenting corrupt
    glare.
The faraway has descended with microscopic intimate
    closeness.
We are losing the swells of courage as dying people sing.
The strong and fortunate live to sing also. What shall we
    sing?

*Brenda Bunting is a Black poet who takes her audience on her
journey between the intersections of being a woman, an
African American, and an environmentally and socially
conscious advocate. She's the author of "Poems of Love and
Violence in Between Life and Death"- 1st and 2nd Editions on
Amazon.*

Fight Not Flight

Sharon Brummer – Mossel Bay, Western Cape, South Africa

Listless, confused?
Revert to logic
Knowledge pierces holes in scaremongering
Bravery punches holes in anxiety
Swim, stroke by stroke
Breathe, deep breaths
Stand tall, do not fall

Numbers swept up in the wind
Deaths versus lives
Politicians counting
Look around you
Listen in the silence
Smell the clean air
Life is happening

Surrealism offers up a virus
Attacking human armory
Be a warrior
Prevail and gather life's tools
Stand and fight
Darkness will become light

Sharon Brummer is a published author and poet. She writes various genres including children's books, intrigue, romance, thriller, and poetry. She lives in the Western Cape, South Africa.

May 2020

Sheila McEntee – Charleston, West Virginia, USA

"It was another day in my history of posthumous days, another day when nobody touched my body."
—From "Stained" by West Virginia Poet Laureate Irene McKinney

I wake in the night and find my dog stretched across the bed. Curled on my left side, I occupy but a sliver of mattress. I get up to use the bathroom, and when I return, I cannot nestle in without nudging him.

"Move over, pal," I say softly, pushing him gently with my knees. As I turn over, he stands for a moment, then curls down against my body, his back pressed to mine. In minutes, we're both asleep.

In the morning, I find him stretched parallel to me, his head resting on my thigh. Bleary eyed, I rise up on one elbow.

"Good morning, Murph," I say. "How's my sweet potato? How's my sugar boy?"

His warm, brown eyes brighten and his tail thumps the covers soundly, like a woman in the old days beating dirt out of a carpet.

Sitting up, I stroke his head and then bend to bury my face in the thick, soft fur around his neck.

"You smell good," I tell him, and he does, like baked earth and spring grass. I rub his paws, lifting one to my nose. It's warm. It smells good, too, like toasted nuts.

I rub his belly and tug on the floppy triangles of his ears, feeling their velvet softness on the tender skin between my fingers. I turn his ear flaps over, where the skin is bare and pink, like peony petals, and plant a kiss on each one.

In that moment, I am a little girl again, with my arms wrapped around the neck of Scotty, a small, black dog my father got from a man who claimed the puppy was a Scottish terrier. Scotty was more of a rat terrier, we learned, and he had bad habits, like chewing dirty laundry left on the floor, especially underwear. But I loved him all the same. I called him "Lover Boy."

"Stop kissing that damn dog," my father told me time and again. My father worried. It was the era of scarlet fever, measles, and, God forbid, polio. Who knew how children contracted these dreadful diseases?

Now, more than ever, I understand my father's fear. Still, I do not—cannot—stop kissing the dog.

Global: 4,342,565 cases; 296,690 deaths
National: 1,389,935 cases; 84,059 deaths
West Virginia: 67,110 tested; 1,404 positive; 64,330 negative; 59 deaths
The Charleston Gazette-Mail, *May 14, 2020*

Some mornings I wake with the startling knowledge that I have not been touched by another person in weeks. Every cell of my body cries out for it, a keening at dawn.

I was in a relationship, but it ended before all this began. I am no stranger to being alone, but always before, there were close friends to hug hello and goodbye. There were warm kisses on the cheek. There were spring visits to my daughter's house, when we planted impatiens and geraniums in bright pots, drank coffee, and talked while our dogs played in the yard. There were visits with my son when we talked for hours over a beer or two. He helped me paint and move furniture, and then we talked some more. Always I could wrap my arms around my children and my children-in-law, and feel the comfort of their arms around me.

"I mourn these precious times we will never regain," a friend writes in an e-mail. Her father is 96 and sheltering in place with her brother on the farm where she grew up. She longs to see his smile, sit on the front porch swing, and hear the music of the nearby creek.

"Oh, I understand," I write in reply.

"Dr. Anthony Fauci, the nation's top infectious disease expert, plans to issue a stark warning to the Senate this morning over the dangers of reopening the country's economy too swiftly. Fauci said ... that doing so could result in 'needless suffering and death.'"
—The New York Times, On Politics, *May 12, 2020*

A friend of a friend has died, not from the coronavirus but from brain cancer. I'd met him on several occasions. He was a warm, engaging man. He always had a smile. Doctors told him that only one percent of those with his cancer survive.

"I will be in that one percent," he told the doctors. He was a very successful businessman. He knew how to aim high.

But in the end, he fell short. Because of concerns about the virus, his family was not allowed at his bedside until the very end.

I sit quietly on my couch and absorb the sad news. My sacrifices shrink in the wake of bitter cruelties others endure.

"As more virus research has emerged, the outdoors has begun to look safer ... Besides the research, something else has begun to make the outdoors seem more attractive. People have started to go stir crazy. This combination is leading to a surge of new expert advice that might be boiled down to: Get out."
—The New York Times, Morning Newsletter, *May 14, 2020*

My friend Martha calls and says she is in town just overnight. She invites me for a hike with our friend Midge.

"I'd love to go," I say, "but we'll have to socially distance."

"Whatever," Martha replies.

I've known Martha a long time. She lives more dangerously than I do. She lets her dogs lap leftover gravy and sauce directly from the pans. She pays little attention to food expiration dates. She pulls tall poke weeds out of her yard and sautés and eats them. Her husband does not partake.

Once, years ago, when Martha still lived around the corner, I called her at four in the morning because I was afraid I was having a heart attack. Deep down, I knew I wasn't, but I needed reassurance. I needed someone who would not be filled with fear and tell me I should go to the emergency room—now.

In minutes, Martha was at my door. She made us both a cup of tea. She sat with me on the couch until dawn came and my stress pains left. She made me feel I could trust myself.

"Sometimes a cup of tea and a friend are all you need," she said, her arms open wide.

"What is all this juice and all this joy?"
—From "Spring" by Gerard Manley Hopkins, English Jesuit poet

And now we are in the woods, three old friends and our dogs. Martha chose this trail because she knows larkspur blooms here. Walking single file and rarely six feet apart, we spy the rosy-red, starlike blooms of fire pink nestled near the ground amid the leaf litter. Midge uses her walking stick to point out sorrel, its tiny, pink-purple flowers rising above cloverlike leaves brushed with blood-red trim.

May apples cover the forest floor, some in showy, snow-white bloom. Others display the tiny, green, oval-shaped "apple" for which the plant is named.

Hiding in the shade, amid a trio of broad, green leaves, is a stunning jack-in-the-pulpit with deep-maroon stripes. I say that Jack looks jaunty, as he peeks out from beneath the flap dipped rakishly over his head. Midge and Martha laugh.

In a way, the forest makes us giddy, like children. Hearing the voice of a towhee, Martha and I lift our heels up and shuffle back and forth, mimicking the way the bird rustles up leaf matter while foraging on the ground. We laugh some more.

As we walk, the woods ring with wood thrush flute song. The calls of a wood pewee and a red-eyed vireo can barely be heard amid the loud pronouncements of Carolina wrens and cardinals.

Then, as the trail dips down, we find larkspur in abundant bloom. Each flower has a long spur at the back that reminds me of a witch's hat, or perhaps a unicorn horn. Indeed, the blossoms are every bit as magical.

Close to two hours later, having forgotten about the virus, we emerge at the trailhead. We do not tarry. Martha has a long drive home. We pause for but a moment, exchange conspiratorial glances, and then hug one another. Our embraces feel clandestine, and they are all too brief.

"If people see us, they'll say we're crazy," Midge says. "We're breaking the law!"

But there are no witnesses, only a rose-breasted grosbeak offering its sweet, fluid song from the branches of a towering beech.

Sheila McEntee writes frequently about nature and her home. Her essays have appeared in the Brevity *magazine nonfiction blog;* Voices on Unity: Coming Together, Falling Apart; *and* Wonderful West Virginia *magazine, among other publications, and aired on West Virginia Public Radio. She lives in Charleston, West Virginia.*

Government Health Warning

Rebecca Lowe – Swansea, South Wales, United Kingdom

Stop—Don't touch—
These fingers breed
dangerous caresses

Kisses are contagion,
spilling fevers from
treacherous lips;
Trust no-one

Love is viral, sweeping
through cities, leaving none
immune—so avoid
the collision of closeness

Make sure to keep
your breaths calm and even,
Do not elevate heartrate,
Such physical symptoms
might arouse suspicion.

Douse yourself daily with
Alcohol, to stifle sensation,
Do not risk honesty,
Quarantine your emotions
safely behind sanitised walls.

Do not dance
Do not share a microphone
Do not hold hands
or stand in close proximity:
Always be on your watch.

Secrete yourself safely
behind the anonymity of screens,
Where the truth cannot touch you,
And love cannot catch.

Rebecca Lowe *is a poet and performer based in Swansea, South Wales. She co-runs Talisman Spoken Word open mic. Her poetry has been featured on BBC Radio 4's Poetry Workshop. Her first collection of poetry,* Blood and Water, *is due for publication in November 2020 with* The Seventh Quarry Press.

Food Soldiers

Setjhaba Ernest Moleko – Vereeniging, Gauteng, South Africa

As a writer of narrative non-fiction, no work is beneath or above me. Any work I do is full of lessons and experiences I can use later in my writings. I have since discovered that work, any kind of work, gives my writing shape, form, and a life of its own. I'm happiest when I'm reflecting on my real life experiences and that of people around me.

When the Corona virus started, most of my colleagues and I spent six days a week at Four Way KwikSpar, trying our best to make an honest living. A majority of us had heard about COVID-19, but since it was still in Asia and Europe, most of us thought it was too far away to have a direct impact on us. People in South Africa made jokes about it on social media and in real life. Little did we know the world is interconnected, and whatever happens in other countries has a direct impact on our own. This we had to learn the hard way.

When the government announced there were fellow South Africans living in China where the virus was at its thickest who had to be repatriated back to the country, people began panic. In the midst of all the confusion, fake news and unfounded opinions about COVID-19 took form.

The South African government felt the need to clear the air and provide relevant and reliable information. Like other countries affected by the outbreak, South Africa suffered a devastating effect to its economy due to the national lockdown that was put in place to curb the spread of the virus. Businesses closed their doors and people lost their jobs. Worried, many South Africans stayed indoors.

All had not been lost, it seemed, because for many South African parents, the national lockdown meant spending time with their children and getting to know them better on a different level. It gave people time to reflect on their lives and where they saw themselves in the future. It gave artists like me time to work on various projects in solitude. However, I have also been very busy serving the community by ensuring there is enough food.

Before the virus, I was just a stubborn, broke writer trying to earn a living at a job to support what I was really passionate about—writing. Keeping a regular job meant having limited time to write, as I spent all my time at work.

Little did I know that I would soon change from a supermarket worker to an 'essential service worker' in a space of about two and a half months. After that radical change of job title, I felt almost like a soldier in battle—except the enemy my colleagues and I are fighting is an invisible one. Our weapon of choice is food and essential items, ensuring they are available for the public during these testing times.

Setjhaba Ernest Moleko has a degree in Public Relations and Communication from the University of Johannesburg. He is a devoted writer and a keen student of life and all it has to teach. He found his passion for writing through reading. He currently works as a butchery assistant at a supermarket.

Silver Lining

Aaron R. – Arlington, Virginia, USA

President initially thought it was a joke
Corporations struggling and going broke
Churches starting to lose hope
Conspiracy theorists saying "stay woke"

Call corona an epidemic
Call COVID-19 a pandemic
Everyone can relate because
the whole world is dealing with it

Just because we are supposed to distance ourselves socially
That doesn't mean we can't speak
Schools are closed but that doesn't mean we can't teach
Churches are closed but that doesn't mean we can't preach
Nobody said it would be easy but this is the feat
And if we somehow come together we will never see defeat

I know, it's easier said than done, but if we alter our minds
The best lessons in life are learned after some of the
toughest and roughest times
And after the darkest times is when the sun starts shining
We have to keep on grinding, keep on trying
I know it's hard when people are dying
But eventually, we'll find the silver lining

*Aaron R. is an award-winning poet. He also produces, edits,
and records his own poetry videos.*

How COVID-19 Impacted My Life

Precious Maluleka (age 13) – Midrand, Gauteng, South Africa

"2020 is going to be a great year!" said many people on New Year's Eve. Well, we've been at home since 26 March here in South Africa. That's around 150 days (as of August 11, 2020), and it's all because of the COVID-19 pandemic. At first, I was excited because we couldn't go to school. It's not because I dislike school or anything—I was just glad I didn't have to wake up early every morning or do a lot of schoolwork. I thought I'd get to watch television all day long. I thought I'd be able to eat a snack whenever I wanted without anyone shouting, "Wait for lunch time! You can't be eating during class!"

No. That was not the case. In fact, it was quite the opposite. We spent a lot of time cleaning and doing other chores, so I barely got a chance to watch TV. I cannot just eat whatever, whenever I wanted to, because we shouldn't go out a lot buying things that aren't necessary, and my favourite snacks aren't exactly "essential." Last and certainly the worst is that I don't get to see my friends. I miss them so much. All our plans for the holidays disappeared as if they were never made. It's just so boring. Every day is just like the last. Not to mention a myriad of people getting infected and dying from this ghastly virus. In South Africa, there are currently 567,740 confirmed cases, and over 10,000 people have lost their lives. It may even be more now, depending on when you are reading this.

But during this time, I remembered something. I remembered all the times my friends and I wished it were the holidays so we didn't have to go to school, wishing I were too sick to be sent to the nearest shop to buy bread so I could stay home. Now I wish I could go to school or walk to the store. I'm going to be more careful about what I wish for, because it might just come true.

I soon realized this wasn't going to end anytime soon, and complaining about it wasn't helping, so I decided to make the best of this time. I used things that were lying around the house to entertain myself. I painted a few mugs and sold them to my parents. My school started online classes, so I still wake up early every day, but it's nothing I'm not already used to. And I appreciate that I'm able to continue with my schoolwork and studying during this time.

I've been doing a whole lot of things. I painted and drew a lot of murals, I painted my room, I learnt how to play the piano using my aunt's old keyboard, I started cooking exotic recipes for my family, and I even started learning French through YouTube. I've always wanted to do all of these, but I just didn't have the time to explore them—but now I do.

I'm taking advantage of this situation, and I encourage you to do so too. I have never felt this good. I started eating healthier, I exercise more, and I started meditating and doing yoga. I feel great, and even though I don't get to see my friends or go to the movies, I appreciate everything I have now.

I will never take going outside, shaking people's hands, or hugging others for granted, because I know what it feels like not to be able to do any of those. "People say you don't know what you've got until it's gone. Truth is, you knew what you had, you just never thought you'd lose it" [Clarissa Wild, Author].

In this time, I pray for everybody who has been affected by this virus in any way. Essential service workers put their lives at risk every day for us, and I believe they deserve a lot of respect. I know we will recover from this; let's all play our part and follow regulations. COVID-19 will not be the end of us!

Precious Maluleka is a thirteen-year-old living in South Africa. She loves cooking, writing stories, drawing, painting, playing piano, and gardening. She also loves reading and learning new things.

Mother's Day Zoom

Patricia McAlpine – Warwick, Rhode Island, USA

Mother's Day, not quite the same.
No buffet brunches, no family gatherings
except on Zoom.

We gathered from our respective homes—
son, daughters, grandchildren, great-grandchildren.
Mom rather puzzled and bemused
to see us all in small frames
like *Hollywood Squares,* a game show
she would know.

Each of us wished her a Happy Mother's Day
Even her cat Gracie was there in the room,
in a place called Zoom.

Patricia McAlpine has been writing poetry for many years. She finds inspiration in nature and family. She currently works as Marketing Associate in for the Blackstone Valley Tourism Council in which she uses her writing skills in writing and curating their bi-monthly newsletter and tourism blog.

Spoofing Shakespeare During the Pandemic

John Dutton – Woodbridge, Virginia, USA

Macbeth

ACT V SCENE I
Dunsinane. Ante-room in the castle.

[*Enter* a **Doctor of Physic** and a **Waiting-Gentlewoman**]

Doctor
I have two nights watched with you, but can perceive no truth in your report. When was it she last coughed?

Gentlewoman
Since his majesty went into the field, I have seen her rise from her bed, throw her nightgown upon her, unlock her closet, take forth paper, fold it, write upon't, read it, afterwards seal it, and again return to bed; yet all this while coughing her bloody head off.

Doctor
A great perturbation in nature, to receive at once this great sickness of COVID-19, and do nothing towards the effects of it besides watching! In this contagious agitation, besides her coughing and other actual performances, what, at any time, have you heard her say?

Gentlewoman
That, sir, which I will not report after her.

Doctor
You may to me: and 'tis most meet you should.

Gentlewoman
Neither to you nor anyone; having no witness to confirm my speech, for I trust no one in these dark days.

[*Enter* **LADY MACBETH** with a taper]

Lo you, here she comes! See with your own eyes the depths of her decay. Observe her; stand close.

Doctor
How came she stay upright with all that hacking?

Gentlewoman
Why, it stood by her: she has Robitussin flowing through her continually; 'tis her command.

Doctor
You see, her bloodshot eyes are open in slits; she looks comatose.

Gentlewoman
Ay, but her sense of smell is shut.

Doctor
What is it she does now? Look, how she rubs her hands.

Gentlewoman
It is an accustomed action with her, to seem thus washing her hands in sanitizer: I have known her continue in this a quarter of an hour.

LADY MACBETH
Yet here's a spot.

Doctor
Hark! she speaks: I will set down what comes from her, to satisfy my remembrance the more strongly.

LADY MACBETH
Out, damned contagion! Out, I say!—One: two: why, then,
'tis time to do 't.—Hell is murky!—Fie, COVID-19, fie!
Disease, and virus be gone! What need I fear who knows it,
when none can call our President to account?—Yet who
would have thought I have so much of the germ on me.

Doctor
Do you mark that?

LADY MACBETH
The grocer at Giant had toilet paper: where is it now?—
What, will these hands ne'er be clean?—No more o' that, my
President, no more o' that: you mar all with this starting.

Doctor
Go to, go to; you have known what you should not.

Gentlewoman
She has spoke what she should not, I am sure of that: heaven
knows what she has known.

LADY MACBETH
Here's the smell of the sanitizer still: all the sanitizers of
Arabia will not cure this little hand. Oh, oh, oh!

Doctor
What a sigh is there! The health is sorely charged.

Gentlewoman
I would not have such a heart in my bosom for the dignity of
the whole body.

Doctor
Well, well, well—

Gentlewoman
Pray God it be, sir.

Doctor
This disease is beyond my practise: yet I have known those
which have even coughed in their sleep who have died holily
in their beds.

LADY MACBETH
Wash your hands, put on your nightgown; look not so
pale.—I tell you yet again, Banquo's buried; he cannot come
out on's grave and spread the virus further.

Doctor
Even so?

LADY MACBETH
To bed, to bed! there's knocking at the gate: come, come,
come, come, give me your hand. What's done cannot be
undone.—To bed, to bed, to bed!

[Exit]

Doctor
Will she go now to bed?

Gentlewoman
Directly.

Doctor
Foul whisperings are abroad: unnatural deeds
Do breed unnatural troubles: infected mouths
To their deaf pillows will discharge their secrets:
More needs she the divine than the physician.
God, God forgive us all! Look after her;
Remove from her the means of all annoyance,
And still keep eyes upon her. So, good night:

My mind she has mated, and amazed my sight.
I think, but dare not speak.

Gentlewoman
Good night, good doctor.

John Dutton *has taught language arts to middle school students in Prince William County for more years than he can remember. He hosts Spilled Ink VA, an open microphone night celebrating the written word. John has published three books:* Armadillo Lost Her Pillow, Argument at the Airport, *and* Billy Pug's Bad Day.

Quarantine Blues

Brittany Sabatino – Washington, DC, USA

Stay indoors and save lives;
It all sounds so simple.
But they don't say how hard
Love is during quarantine.

I miss the outdoors
And the mornings I would jog
In both a state of misery and bliss.

I miss my youngest niece
And the chubby baby face
I would cover in kiss after kiss.

I miss my nephew
And all his witty comebacks;
Oh the games we would play.

I miss my three older nieces
Sitting on my lap
With their sweet and kind way.

I miss coffee dates
And the potential memories;
Hope of caffeine magic.

I miss my freedom.
With limited possibilities,
Love becomes tragic.

Brittany Sabatino *is a poet living in the Washington, DC, area and works in the Information Technology field. She has been writing for years but only recently began sharing her writing publicly. She has been published by Thirteen Myna Birds, Scarlet Leaf Publishing, and Spilled Ink Poetry Anthology.*

The Corona

Rodica Todd – Seaford, East Sussex, United Kingdom

I am lonely in my house,
With no cat or dog or mouse.
While I worry for myself
I keep searching the top shelf
For the photos of the past,
All are dead, I am the last
Father, husband still alive,
Bold and willing to survive.

You might ask me why I cry.
I look at the tree and try
To make sense of just one word,
The 'Corona.' With its sword
Kills the People of this planet.
This is how I lost my Janet,
And my little girl and boy,
I am left with just one toy,
To remember they were here,
On the swing. The tree is near
Their ashes, deeply drowned
In the tears underground.

I am lonely in my house,
On the tablet I could browse
The whole world with pain and strife.
Miss my dad and mum and wife.

I am locked behind the walls,
Cold, I put on hats and shawls.

Outdoors COVID stopped its stroll.
It's time now to find the toll

Of the people who have left.
Isolated and bereft,
I decide to watch the news,
I am stunned! A change of views:
"Better summer than the spring!"
I pick up the phone to ring,
Tell the world. I start to sing!
End the bad dream of the night,
It is morning, warm and bright!

Then I realise, awake,
My Life has to have a Break.
If I want to rid of Spikes.
I must share, get the 'likes',
The 'thumb up' from all my friends,
Trusting that this COVID ends.
"One for all and all for one,"
Fight the COVID and be done!

A nightmare from the deep,
Had my soul, while fast asleep.
I can see—I'm not that blind—
That the worst was in my mind.
Mum and Dad are still with us,
Kids have breakfast without fuss,
Janet sends a smile to them—
I love her, she is my gem.

Then with all of us around,
We stay happy, safe and sound.
The new dawn brought us much light,
And the HOPE we'll be all right.

Rodica Todd, *of Seaford, England, says, "Writing about COVID-19 is like juggling with Misfortune and Fortune at the same time. When the whole world seems to crumble, there are ways to bring it together again: by sharing love and positivity."*

Original art by Rodica Todd

"Corona" is a scary foe. Take a seat on the chair, look outside the window, then up. The open blue sky will free you from black thoughts. Life, in red, will touch the green fields of Hope, fight against COVID, and win. (Ink and acrylic on textured paper, 15 cm x 15 cm).

Another COVID Ball

Lana Hunneyball – West Sussex, United Kingdom

My life has been one big, beautiful, curved ball from the moment my mother was given the wrong baby.

"That's not my baby," she cried.

The nurse must have assumed the trauma of childbirth had stripped my mother of her maternal instincts and tried to nudge the precious bundle into her arms. "Of course it is, dear. Don't worry, everything will be okay."

"It's not my damn child!"

The nurse's eyes widened. Now where does a sixties housewife in South Africa get such unnatural confidence? "Look, madam, here is her little armband. *Baba Maitland,"* she read, as if that settled the matter.

"I don't care. Mine had ten strands of white hair coming from her crown." My mother's lip quivered. "Go away and find my baby."

I often wonder what life might have been like if my mother didn't have the observational skills of a reconstructive surgeon, which was what she'd wanted to be, but went to art school and fell pregnant instead. Ah, history, you cry from the gaping wound of unfulfilled potential!

Not that she didn't become a spectacular artist, but that's another story. I'm extremely grateful to her, especially as about eight months before, she'd enquired about a termination. At the last minute she changed her mind and walked out of the doctor's office.

Somewhere in my teens, my mom gave me a birthday card that read: "If it's true that people learn from their mistakes, then you must be one of the cleverest people I know." My adult life has been one 'shouldn't have' after another. I shouldn't have fallen pregnant in third year varsity—shouldn't have gotten married knowing it was a mismatch—shouldn't have become a housewife instead of a psychologist. But Life gave me two beautiful daughters and myriad precious moments. I ran my own business designing communication and training materials, started a trust for HIV orphans, and much more besides. I was even a professional clown for a while. Along the way I developed my love affair with words and their exquisite power.

Lockdown gave me time to reflect on all my shouldn't haves.

Shouldn't have stayed married, but my husband was a truly good man. Shouldn't have sacrificed my health. Shouldn't have finally left when I did—mid shitstorm, broken, dotage looming. Shouldn't have plunged into gypsy wanna-be-writerhood, deeper ill health, and a bunch more shouldn't haves.

Through it all, a single awareness kept me going: I was birthing, being pressed into being, like a pearl or a diamond. Every mistake I made, every time I let go of attachment to outcome with grace, I was being guided along a birth canal to something more fantastic and beautiful than I could imagine. What, I did not know. A thread of faith seemed to link my chaotic serendipities into a necklace that was me.

So on March 14, 2020, I 'shouldn't have' boarded one of the last planes to squeak into the USA before borders closed. Two years before, I had moved to the UK. Unintentionally, of course. I came over to make money as a live-in carer [caregiver]—enough to keep the wolf from the door and leave me in bloody peace to write.

When I got here, it was a slam-dunk—I was staying. Why claw desperately for every penny if you don't have to? Even though my beloved home country, South Africa, gave less than a proverbial crap for my existence, I felt like a turncoat abandoning it just as corruption spread like a fiery bacterial monster eating itself. Until it dawned on me that I can't do anything useful if I'm not okay.

Two years on, I'm balancing caring stints amongst the writing, and it's hard. When you're knee-deep in diarrhea after ten days of fifteen-hour shifts, it's easy to wonder how the hell it came to this. *I shouldn't be here.* But these are just birthing pains.

Halfway through a caring stint with my client—a quadriplegic woman in her seventies—my daughter called from the USA. Her husband was on long deployment with the navy, and his return had been delayed, courtesy of COVID. Faced with the prospect of lockdown with a radioactive five-year-old son and no hubby, she was unravelling.

It's a fine line, knowing when to leave them to their life lessons or jump in when the chips are down. I assessed the cost-benefit of her being stuck indefinitely on her own versus me being stuck there with no guarantee when I'd be back, and did what mothers do.

There would be a cost. I'd just found three months' accommodation in London in lieu of thirty hours care work per month. It was perfect! At last I wouldn't be scuffling from one Airbnb or friend to another between work shifts, dragging my suitcase like that woman in *Baghdad Café*. Perhaps I could even start tacking my health back together.

These days, when things don't go my way, I barely miss a beat, but it was with a heavy sigh that I unpacked my newly acquired car and stacked (some of) the crap I'd collected since being in the UK back into my client's loft.

I still had a week to prepare for the trip, and who knows, COVID might be over in a month and I'd be back in my cosy nest (yeah, right). On the last day of my shift, tired but wired, I walked into my new room, put my new duvet cover onto my new duvet, made a cup of tea, and Skyped my daughter to see how things were going.

"They're closing the borders, Mom. You have to come tomorrow."

It was seven p.m. I downed my tea and, per miracle, managed to change my ticket for the following morning. It took an hour or so to cram my worldly possessions into orange recycling bags and stash them under my bewildered landlady's musty staircase and apologise for letting her down. Another hour to drag myself to friend Tanya's on the other side of London, because getting to Heathrow by four a.m. from here would be a nightmare.

After a bath, soul-sister ruminations on the vagaries of life, and a few hours' sleep, I arrived at Hammersmith bus station, bleary-eyed. The shops declared their wares to abandoned passages under neon lights. With COVID fresh on the collective super-conscious, even the "chavs and hooligans" that notoriously lurk here at night seemed to have gone to ground.

There was one woman, sitting on a metal chair and tapping her phone. "The tube is down," her voice echoed. The accent was South American.

"Well, how do I get to Heathrow?"

"Which terminal?"

"I don't know. Delta airlines?"

"Ah, follow me, I work for them."

Whenever I really need something, it appears. I used to think everyone's life was like that, but apparently, it's not. Or maybe it is, and people just don't listen or notice.

I got to the gate at Heathrow Terminal Four just as fifty or so people were boarding. I had been re-assigned to business class, and on the plane, there was not a soul around me. The one place I was *not* going to get COVID was on this plane. The layover in Charlottesville felt like a scene from *I Am Legend*.

To be fair, the waiting area filled up a bit. There was an air of smug camaraderie from having squeaked through before the borders closed, but it wasn't anything like the havoc portrayed on the newscasts. No one knew what to expect, so we hunkered down behind our masks and made COVID small talk peppered with silly jokes.

After crossing five time zones, my UK winter body stumbled into a deserted Jacksonville airport, oppressive Florida heat, and the arms of my grateful child. Well, we didn't actually touch. I was on a fourteen-day no touching, kissing, or going-out ban. Try telling that to an excited five-year-old who hasn't seen his granny for a year.

In the short time I'd been in the air, COVID had turned the world upside down.

My friend Bill and I agreed to keep each other sane via Skype. Bill is a struggling Mick Jagger look-alike muso living in Cape Town. Within a short time, to my utter surprise, our friendship blossomed into the possibility of something else.

After two months, my son-in-law's return was delayed yet again. Although the borders coming into the US were closed, repatriation to the UK was allowed. Summoning faith that this would not change, I postponed my return. Things got tense. My daughter feared she'd never see her husband again, and radioactive five-year-olds are unaware of the whims of the system—except, of course, they act out even more when adults are stressed.

About two weeks later, I received an automated email from the US government along the lines of, "We do hope you've enjoyed your stay, but you must be gone in ten days."

What? I thought my ESTA visa was valid for six months. Why didn't I check? What is wrong with me? It was out of my hands, but my daughter was at breaking point. Why was everything falling apart so spectacularly?

That afternoon, I sat in the sunroom reading. There's no point fighting something you can't change. Next thing, my phone rang. It was a WhatsApp call from my son-in-law, who, being on deployment, is hard pushed to find a way to talk to his wife, never mind unimportant mothers-in-law!

The first thing he asked was, "Are you out of earshot of your daughter?"

"Yes," I said. "What's wrong?" My heart raced as I feared the worst: He was delayed again and didn't know how she would handle it.

"I'm coming home tomorrow."

Just like that—the baton was wielded. It was one of those moments that confirmed my belief that there is definitely a strange and beautiful pattern to this life.

"Dude, you literally have absolutely no idea how glad I am to hear that."

He wanted me to take the phone to my grandson so he could tell him, so my grandson could tell my daughter. (My son-in-law's sense of humour can be disturbing!)

"You won't be popular," I warned.

"It'll be fine. Can you do it secretly?"

My grandson was in the bath, so after some fancy footwork about wanting to help and telling my daughter to go and have a nice cup of tea, I embarked on the secret mission.

It sort of worked, but when my grandson blurted out, "Daddy's coming home!" my daughter thought he was losing it too and burst into tears.

"It's true," I said, and handed her the phone.

She fell to the ground, sobbing. It had been seven months. Of course, he got an earful for his choice of delivery, but what I was seeing was the Godiverse at his/her/its best: creating beauty out of chaos.

I went back to my room and sat in awe of the timing; reminded myself that it was true: I *had* received the email that morning and my precious family would be reunited the very next day.

It's these kinds of things that happen to me often enough that I don't question anymore.

A few days later, I was back in the UK. Three months on, the borders are still closed. Bill and I still chat regularly. Except for lockdown, I might never have discovered the depths of this rich soul. I have no idea how this particular 'shouldn't have' will pan out, and that's okay. My life continues to string me together with exquisite serendipities, and I'm grateful for every moment.

***Lana Hunneyball** is a South African living in the UK and works as a live-in caregiver. She is working on a novel and other projects. She lives by the Erich Fromm quote, "Life is giving birth to yourself," and works daily to trust the still small voice. Her first poetry collection* Flotsam and Jetsam *will be published shortly.*

Virus

Erika Luzader – Parkersburg, West Virginia, USA

"Virus" is a 9 x 12 watercolor painting on mixed media paper. The inspiration came from how much COVID-19 has impacted daily life.

Erika Luzader is a self-taught artist. Her mediums of choice are minor animations, pixel art, digital art, watercolor paintings, and ink wash. She says: "From the moment I picked up a pencil and started drawing, I knew it was what I wanted to do for the rest of my life."

Trading Stressors

Daphne Tarango – Lakeland, Florida, USA

Since the COVID-19 pandemic started to blanket the world, I've taken more time-outs than usual, sitting quietly in my bedroom and collecting myself before rejoining the craziness that is my home. Two adults, three kids, three dogs, and two cats.

When the number of positive cases in our state and county spiked, anxiety crept in and slumped on my chest. The pressure was so intense I burst into tears and hid in my room. This time-out was different. My hubby slid the pocket door to our bedroom shut and lay on the bed next to me.

After some discussion, we uncovered the source of my increasing panic: The news. I let myself obsess over the flood of information sweeping into our home and hearts. I allowed myself to be sucked in by all the sources, viewpoints, and conspiracy theories. Listening to press conferences intensified a drive in me to "join the conversation" among true—or self-proclaimed—experts.

But it wasn't just the amount of information—and the various viewpoints—I was exposing myself to. The seeming randomness of the virus was—and still is—unsettling. What if I'm in the group of people who gets it? What if my immune system is compromised? What if I come in contact with someone who has it? What if . . . ?

This coronavirus isn't just novel in name. It's novel in its stealth. It made me feel helpless. If I didn't follow precautions, I could get it, and if I did follow precautions, I still could get it. That alone was enough for me to downward spiral—without even noticing it.

Since then, we've distanced and redirected our attention. First, we turned off the constant barrage of news. We check numbers periodically and tune into more state news, focusing on our local officials' response to any developments.

The night my guard crumbled, we turned on something a little more serene. At first, my children scoffed at the idea of watching a program about a family living on a farm in Minnesota in the late 1800s. But they stuck with it and seemed to enjoy it. I enjoyed showing off my knowledge of who was who in the show, what they were like, and how they were related to the family on the prairie.

The laughter was a much-needed break.

We've played board games and practical jokes; designed each other's "Quarantine Hair," played jazz, classical, and worshipful music; searched for lizards with the dogs; watched online events; and harassed the cats with laser pointers. I've also been careful to take my medications on time every time. Can't mess with chemistry!

I hadn't felt pressure on my chest for a while since we'd started distancing from potential stressors and redirecting our attention and energy to less stressful endeavors.

It seemed harmless enough—until all the games, challenges, movies, cooking, videomaking—all the "busy-ness"—started to drain me. At the beginning of the quarantine, I was eager to tackle projects, take on new hobbies—just something, anything to minimize my exposure to the news, pass the time, and be productive. The barrage of ideas on social media soon morphed from helpful to overwhelming. I saw ads and specials for a course here, a workshop there. All great things I would, under other circumstances, take interest in.

But something didn't feel quite right about it—all the productivity talk during a pandemic.

At first, I subscribed to the productivity mindset, but as time dragged on, my motivation dwindled. I actually felt guilty about my lack of productivity. I'd stopped doing a lot of the things I started doing to distract me from the pandemic. Good things! I just didn't have the energy to keep them up.

Reducing one type of stressor to engage in "busy-ness" has been counterproductive. Few people are in the right mindset to spend considerable time on self-help activities, projects, and professional development. Many of us are uncertain about our jobs, family circumstances, daily living—our very existence. These are not times for constant mental, emotional, and physical action for the sake of being productive, adding a skill to a resume, or posting another accomplishment on social media. (Regrettably, I've done all these.) These are times for compassion for ourselves and others.

God doesn't love us more or less based on what we do or don't do. Isn't that a relief? God accepts us not because of how much we've accomplished, but because of His compassion displayed through Jesus Christ, His son. God is the God of compassion—not of false guilt. He is gentle. He doesn't push, and He doesn't drive. He leads and guides. Never with guilt—but with love.

When I crave "busy-ness" to avoid being still, I head to the wooden bench my hubby built for me. It's low to the ground on my front lawn. I soak up the sun as I watch my veggies sprout from the dirt, admire the array of birds stopping by my birdfeeders, or laugh at squirrels hijacking seeds. I take off my shoes and wiggle my feet into the grass. There's something about the pristine and honest qualities of the earth beneath my feet. It's easier for me to ask introspective questions and to answer truthfully. Am I staying busy to avoid . . .

- Interacting with family members?
- Processing hurt feelings, anger, or bitterness?
- Facing low self-worth?
- Spending time with God?

If we are not intentional about managing potential stressors, anxiety can sneak up on us before we realize it. Distancing from those triggers and redirecting our attention is generally a healthy coping mechanism—unless the very things we've turned to overpower us instead.

O that we would trade the stressors of this pandemic—not for other stressors but for peace. O that we would distance ourselves from anything that infects our mind and crushes our heart, and that we would cling to the joys of a serene life with family, friends, and most of all, faith.

Daphne Tarango *comforts others with the comfort she's received from God. She is the author of six books, including* Show Some Love, *a resource for families of loved ones in recovery. Her latest book is* An Unexpected Christmas, *stories of holidays that didn't go as planned. Visit Daphne at DaphneWrites.com.*

Just Today

Myriam Joseph – Cambridge, Massachusetts, USA

Mortgage due, stomach's grumbling
Bill collectors calling and resumés flowing
Can you get help, or were you outsourced?
Will you be okay?

So much pain and uncertainty
Too many doubts; votes, no confidence
What are you doing? Where are you going?
Are you for real?

So many decisions, not enough leaders
Disasters, turmoil, and rebellions
Calls for transparency, no clear answers
Are you moving too slow?

Earth is shattering and water's overhead
Where did that come from?
It happened so fast. How do we fix it?
Can we prevent it? Are you sure?

Myriam Joseph *is a writer and poet based in the Boston area. Her poetry reflects everyday life—its joys and struggles.*

Combine Indoor Walking with Weight Lifting

Sonya Gonzalez – San Antonio, Texas, USA

This is a humorous piece, showing how to adapt to indoor exercising. The figure, wishing to be outdoors, is becoming pale from lack of sunlight. She wears soft, velvet gloves holding a reluctant kitty, who is substituted for weights. The painting is 12" x 12", acrylic on paper mounted on wood.

*Playing the violin at a young age led **Sonya Gonzalez** to painting later in life. Her art is also influenced by the Hispanic culture and nature, and has been featured on the covers of several magazines. She has exhibited locally and nationally and has written and illustrated several books.*

The COVID-19 Stare of Death (fiction)

Gary William Ramsey – Kemah, Texas, USA

I was alone as I walked on the beach that cool April morning. The sound of waves softly rolling to shore and the pleasant ocean breeze gave me a feeling of calm and comfort. I was unaccompanied because everyone I knew was afraid of death from The Virus.

I spotted it in the distance, silhouetted against the off-white sand, its black presence glistening. I knew the entity I was going to face symbolized the wicked COVID-19 Virus. As I approached the malicious adversary, it stood motionless, which was unnatural for a deadly, cowardly foe. They usually hide from human sight and attack your body in a gutless manner. This obstinate Infection just remained there, not moving.

I continued walking until I was five feet away from the brazen Virus. It was blocking my path. I am a human, and I am superior to disease. I will not alter my path for a lowly Virus. It must know its place in the scheme of life and move out of my way.

I called for the Infection to retreat, but it stood firm, while deliberately turning its evil glare toward me. Its black eyes stared ruthlessly into my soul. The stare was merciless and without recognition of my superiority.

The cold chill of fear pierced my consciousness, but I refused to divert from my path. I glared back, determined to break its spirit. I will not remain in my house out of fear of its lethalness.

For an agonizing time, which seemed like infinity, we were locked in mental combat. Its blank, piercing stare pitted against my unrelenting determination.

Finally, after what seemed like an eternity, it showed its invisible cowardice and left our dwelling on earth. I walked to the place where it had stood and defiantly kicked the sand where COVID-19 had left its prints. I refuse to let a Virus beat me. I refuse to let my spirit and my soul die.

This is my world, and a cowardly, invisible Virus will not annihilate it.

Gary William Ramsey enjoyed a highly successful career in retail, achieving the titles of President and CEO of two major U.S. corporations. He lived in 17 different locations in the USA and has traveled to numerous countries around the world. He uses these experiences in his writings. Gary presently resides in Kemah, Texas.

Hold Your Loved Ones Tight

Sharon Brummer – Mossel Bay, Western Cape, South Africa

There's panic
There's confusion
Left or Right?
Hold your loved ones tight

Surrounded by silence
Creativity staunched
We mimic the living
Only love is real

Follow at your peril
Disobey at your expense
There's chaos in the land
Our need for each other boundless

Mere mortals
Choose your path
Madness feeds our world
Gather collective thoughts
An end?
A beginning?
A solution?
Love for humankind save us!

Sharon Brummer *is a published author and poet. She writes various genres including children's books, intrigue, romance, thriller, and poetry. She lives on the Western Cape of South Africa.*

Quarantine Went Like . . . .

Raven Berrian (17 years old) – Henderson, Nevada, USA

The artist states: "This piece literally described my quarantine experience as the last few weeks of my senior year in high school approached. Because my grades were amazing, I was able to not focus on school as much and focus on what I liked to do more, which included Snapchat, Netflix, and Instagram."

Raven Berrian expresses herself through art. She wants to inspire change in the world by touching hearts. She says, "If my art could touch one person every day, I'll know my purpose has been fulfilled."

Love in the Age of COVID

Kayla Bryant – Lakewood, Colorado, USA

If you set your mind to it, you can generally brace for the challenges that come with a long-distance relationship. You can accept that you're not going to have traditional date nights, you're not going to be able to reach for your love's hand anytime you want, and any instance of gazing deeply into each other's eyes will have to take place over FaceTime. You can prepare yourself for that, and you can get advice and support from plenty of couples who have successfully navigated those same waters.

But there is not a soul alive who knows how to prepare you for a long-distance relationship in the middle of a global pandemic.

You might have started off making jokes about social distancing—after all, being over seven hundred miles apart makes you both professionals at this. But as the days went on and the panic levels began to rise, you were both blindsided at how quickly your world changed. You went from expecting a typical final college semester to wondering how your 85-year-old professor is going to navigate the world of video conferencing. He went from feeling burned out at his job to being amazed that he still has one. As you compared notes on how much has happened, you realized you have no idea how to process so many changes in such a short amount of time.

Maybe you two have coped by daydreaming together about the future—what it will be like when you *finally* get to close the gap, your hopes and dreams for your future family, and all the trips you just know you'll be able to take together when this is all done. Instead of gazing into each other's eyes, maybe a few of your FaceTime calls have been simply spent sitting with each other when the air was too heavy for words.

When your mind takes you back to that embrace the last time you dropped him off at the airport, the already bittersweet memory takes on a new level of emotion. You can feel your heart crumbling more and more with each new question. *Did I hug him tight enough that day? When will I be able to hug him again? Will I be able to hug him again?* Maybe you've started praying that you both can feel the warmth of that last embrace until the day comes when you can finally be back in each other's arms.

Dating long-distance when the world has turned upside down was probably the last thing either of you ever expected. However, one thing is for sure: COVID-19 is going to make a remarkable chapter in your love story.

Kayla Bryant *is a native of Denver, Colorado. She is an avid baker and a 2020 graduate of Bear Valley Bible Institute.*

2020 Hindsight

Evie Groch – El Cerrito, California, USA

In my kitchen I make soup,
chicken soup, of course, though
there's no schmaltz in the pantry.
Sorrow boils away in the stockpot,
only a trace of angst left behind
when I add the bird,
weep over a cut onion,
fill the house with silent scents,
swallow the elixir.

During this peculiar pause
we take a step back
to honor old school ways,
to bake with yeast, spring clean till July,
bring out the Singer, stitch in time,
and garden with ardor.

Yet also new steps to learn,
to dance with our deadly partner,
rechoreograph the movement,
let fear pass through.

Wait for a day without death
while I stock up on
servings of compassion
and discover it's
the eighth wonder.

Evie Groch *has been in education all her life, but at a mature age, the love of travel and writing lured her over to the creative side, where she has been published in every genre imaginable. Always up for a challenge, she writes on.*

The Hoarder

Cheryl Kula – Hinton, West Virginia, USA

My entire life, I believed Granny to be a bit of a hoarder. Her pantry held empty plastic butter bowls, with and without lids, stacked in every nook and cranny. Gallon jugs that had initially held milk were stored in the corner containing suspiciously brown-colored water. Beside her kitchen sink, a metal bucket sat on the floor to catch all of the tater peelings and food scraps. The bucket would fill to the top before she would tote it out to one spot in the field behind her house. If she received a kitchen appliance as a gift, but her original appliance still worked, she would save the new one under the bed for when she really needed it. She would shrug us off if we pointed out that the old coffee maker tended to leak or had a weird smell. It still made coffee. It stayed. When I mentioned this to my mother, she would say with a shrug, "Your granny grew up during the Depression. You make do."

Every so often, one of the cousins would be tasked by an aunt to "help Mom clean up." This would mean stuffing a few years' worth of items into trash bags, with Granny clucking behind us as she protested, "I might need those bowls." She would then refuse to speak to the offending person for a couple of weeks.

Her house, however, was where I went when I needed to make something for "crazy hat day" or when I needed help creating an object for a school project. Taking my cousin's ancient GI Joe, Granny redrew his eyes into an Asian slant, then helped me put scraps of fabric together until I had a tiny representative for my project on Emperor Hirohito.

When I moved into my first apartment, I jokingly asked my dad to ask Granny if she had a toaster tucked under the bed that I could have. He arrived with a new toaster and, with a straight face, said, "She said to tell you it was in the closet, not under the bed."

As an adult in my own home, I tossed away items with abandon. In one span of eight years, I had moved eight times because of changes in roommates, boyfriends, and finances. Carrying empty butter bowls from one house or apartment to the next quickly lost appeal, if it had ever had any to start. But finally, I settled with joy into one location and one relationship. Feeling that we were environmentally savvy, we bought a covered tin to save our scraps that eliminated any smells—unlike Granny's bucket—before taking it to our compost pile. But even then, I would surreptitiously toss away a shelf of butter bowls, jelly jars, and huge empty yogurt containers that my husband had stored because we already had shelves crammed with glassware with easy-to-match lids for storage.

And then, COVID-19 arrived. For us, it came on a Friday the thirteenth, when I got the call to pick up the girls from school because they were closing indefinitely. From a quiet life at home, my daily life became a horse of a different color. The packets of schoolwork the school sent as "instruction" was boring busy-work that took the girls less than an hour to complete, but under duress, which was an unacceptable situation to me. I ignored the packets and began to design activities and projects for each subject. Cardboard toilet paper rolls took on an entirely new meaning. My husband raised his eyebrows but made no comment when I feverishly dug them out of trash bags. Empty butter bowls became collection sites for snail shells, crystal-making science experiments, and vats of slime. Stacks of paper I hoarded for my personal writing projects disappeared with frightening speed as the girls practiced math problems and wrote letters, poems, short stories, and essays.

Amid the self-isolation, a project planned before COVID-19 came to fruition. Four beehives arrived, and we scurried to set them up on a beautiful, sunny day. My husband had stashed away empty gallon jugs in a cabinet too high for me to reach. I commandeered them to make gallons of sugar water to feed our fledgling hives. We had been excited about the project before the arrival of COVID-19, but now, working hand-in-hand with Mother Nature gave us a sense of confidence and satisfaction. The world may struggle, but we grasped a moment of control.

I stood one evening at the stove, slowly heating water to dissolve the sugar before putting it into jugs so we could feed the bees. I found my eyes sweeping around the kitchen at the clutter I wouldn't have permitted just a year ago. In one corner, egg cartons were neatly stacked and ready to go up the road to my neighbor from whom we buy eggs. Along the counter, the girls had laid out small painting projects to dry, while the other counter held science experiments-in-progress.

Beside my reading chair beyond the kitchen, three sewing projects littered the end table with slips of thread, a Mason jar full of buttons, and scraps of fabric covering a stack of books and papers. In front of me, behind the stove, a pile of empty butter, sour cream, and cottage cheese containers waited until I could get a stool to store them on a pantry shelf.

I stirred slowly, listening to a momentary precious silence in the house, and stared at those unmatched plastic bowls. I had thought Granny was a hoarder, but my mother was right. Sometimes, you just make do.

Cheryl Kula lives on a mountain in West Virginia with her husband, two daughters, and a variety of four-legged companions. She has published two children's books, Play Day with Daddy, *and* A Different Tail.

What Shall I Always Remember?

Rebecca Lowe – Swansea, South Wales, United Kingdom

That impossibly clear, blue sky,
Not a plane to be seen anywhere,
Roads you could walk down,
Devoid of the choking influence of cars.

How the neighbours left their rooms
And rediscovered the beauty of being outside,
Chalked artwork on walls,
Playing music in the sunshine,
Rainbow pictures in the windows.

How we shared half-smiles
And offered, from a distance,
Assistance to people we'd never
Bothered speaking to before.

How we learned to put our own needs
Behind the health and welfare of others,
How we cheered those who kept everything
Going—doctors, nurses, care workers,
Bin collectors, teachers, shopkeepers.

How, suddenly, the world stopped,
Became smaller, turned inward,
Causing us to rethink and reflect upon
The things that really mattered,
How a wardrobe of fine clothes
Became superfluous, how toilet rolls,
Pasta, and soap became valuable commodities.

How quickly we learned the difference
Between 'want' and 'need,' and how

Disease refuses to discriminate
Between rich and poor.
How plush hotels flung open
Their doors to the homeless.

How the churches closed,
And for the first time,
We prayed like we really meant it,
And God left the building
And hit the streets,

And we fell to our knees
And got on with the sacred task
Of serving one another.

Rebecca Lowe *is a poet and performer based in Swansea, South Wales. She co-runs Talisman Spoken Word open mic. Her poetry has been featured on BBC Radio 4's Poetry Workshop. Her first collection of poetry* Blood and Water *is due for publication in November 2020 with The Seventh Quarry Press.*

Wake

Sheila McEntee – Charleston, West Virginia, USA

I stand at the kitchen sink, washing my hands yet again, when out of the corner of my eye I see a dark shape soaring outside the window. It quickly disappears from sight, but then returns, a hulking mass flying toward the trees. I watch intently now as it rears up, unfolds expansive wings, and lands in near-bare branches. The bird is now unmistakable.

"Turkey vulture," I say out loud as I dry my hands with a damp towel. I've used the towel several times today already. I glance down at my hands and rub them, feeling their sandpaper roughness, noting the raw, bright-pink peaks of my knuckles.

When I glance up again, I see two more enormous birds join the first one; one sidles up on the same branch, while the other settles on a limb nearby.

"How about that?" I say to myself. "A meet-up of vultures."

I know these birds like to gather in groups. So do I, but right now, I'm not allowed to.

Indeed, due to the COVID-19 pandemic, I'm alone a lot more. I also have more time on my dry, chapped hands. I cannot see my friends, but a visit with vultures is still permitted. I go to find my binoculars.

Peering through the lenses, I see tree branches just beginning to sprout. The tender, lime-green leaflets are so small, I easily can see the birds between them.

I find the trio and zero in for an up-close view. Hunched and homely with heads hung low, they grasp the branches with long, pink toes. Their feet are the color of my knuckles and match the birds' pulpy faces, which I imagine look not unlike the entrails they pull from a roadkill opossum or raccoon.

I wonder why they have chosen to gather in my tree. Is there something dead just over the hillside? A deer? Pray not the gray cat that skulks through my yard each day. Neighbors tell of coyotes howling in the night, though I have never heard one. Anyway, a coyote would surely make off with its prey, not leave it.

A quick online search informs me that a group of perching vultures is called a *wake*. I eye them again. With their heavy heads in a close, dark, huddle, they look like mourners. Yet, I learn that, rather than congregating around something dead, the birds may be migrating and just stopping here for a rest.

While I am enthralled with the vultures, two blue jays are not. They mob the larger birds, diving toward them relentlessly, hopping up and down in the surrounding branches, cawing loudly in alarm.

"It's okay. They're not hawks," I reassure them. "They won't steal your babies."

Still, the jays carry on, while the vultures roundly ignore them.

I watch as the big birds settle in. One lumbers along a smooth branch, sidestepping awkwardly as if feeling for the most comfortable spot. Another flexes its unwieldy wings in a wide, cumbersome stretch, then tucks them neatly next to its body. The third lifts a wing and dips its head beneath it, perhaps preening away a bothersome mite. In all this, I notice the birds' easy familiarity with one another, perhaps the kind I have with close friends who know my idiosyncrasies and love me just the same.

I think now of those friends who, like me, are largely isolated in their homes. I think of my children, who live far away. When will I thrill to the sight of them, feel the comfort of their smiles, hug them tight? In this moment I envy the quiet company the vultures keep with one another.

I am reminded that these birds are no strangers to death; nor are we, in this troublesome time. Indeed, one unshielded breath could lead to our last. And if we succumb, there can be no wake or other service where loved ones gather to mourn us. I am grateful to be safe inside, waiting it out, even if alone.

I watch the birds for a long while and then return to my solitary tasks. Under a cloudy sky, backyard life goes on. Squirrels skitter up trees and take no notice of the dark heaps in the branches. A Carolina wren sings loudly. In the distance, a titmouse calls insistently for a mate but gets no reply. The blue jays give up and go about their business.

Sheila McEntee writes frequently about nature and her home. Her essays have appeared in the Brevity *magazine nonfiction blog;* Voices on Unity: Coming Together, Falling Apart; *and* Wonderful West Virginia Magazine, *among other publications, and aired on West Virginia Public Radio. She lives in Charleston, West Virginia.*

COVID Weight

Paige Turner – Auckland, New Zealand

Tried to grow in wisdom
Went up a size instead
COVID weight they called it
COVID weight they said
Booze snacks food
Drink munch fry it
I will just grab lunch
Then I'll start my diet

Paige Turner is a writer who likes to keep her readers guessing right up until the last page. In a global pandemic, she turns to poetry, surprising even herself. She is also a teacher, musician, actor, artist, gardener, cook, and waitress. She lives in Auckland, New Zealand.

Quarantined

Patricia McAlpine – Warwick, Rhode Island, USA

It's like being stuck in a perpetual storm.
You hunker down and don't dare go anywhere.
You stay in the comfort of home
to brace for the wind-driven snow.

But it's springtime
The flowers bloom and birds sing
beckoning you outside to join them
in your backyard and your neighborhood,
the confines of your adventure.
Yet, discoveries are still made
in the wonders of nature.

Back inside you move from
the TV chair to the reading chair
by the window, where books and imagination
take you beyond the news, beyond the world
we now live in—Quarantined.

Patricia McAlpine has been writing poetry for many years. She finds inspiration in nature and family. She currently works as Marketing Associate for the Blackstone Valley Tourism Council in which she uses her writing skills in writing and curating their bi-monthly newsletter and tourism blog.

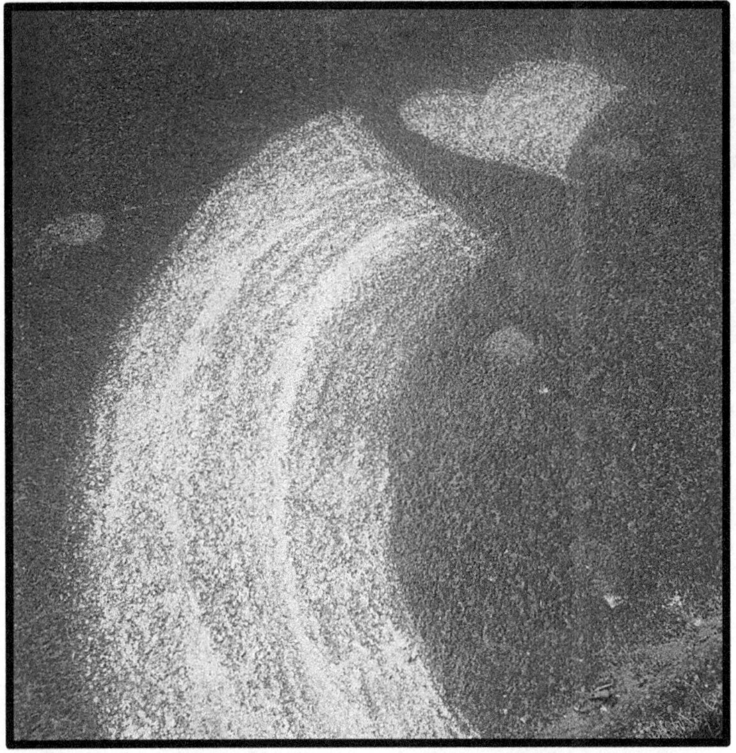

Photograph by Patricia McAlpine

Over Easter weekend, I took a walk through my neighborhood and was inspired by the chalk art reflecting hope during this pandemic, so I snapped this photograph. Walking through my neighborhood was my only refuge, with Rhode Island state parks and community parks in lockdown during this time period.

Pandemic Memoir

Lisa A. McCombs – Monongah, West Virginia, USA

Diagnosed with multiple sclerosis in 2001, I have become increasingly reclusive over the years, so when COVID-19 decided to visit the USA, things didn't change drastically for me.

Or, so I thought.

Suddenly, I missed a social life I hadn't realized existed.

My COVID-19 journey began in late February 2020. My parents and I planned to visit Dad's sister in the state capital where she resided. Any time I have a book event there, we take advantage of the opportunity to spend time with her. Retired and alone, she usually welcomed us with open arms. I enjoyed these visits. A self-proclaimed career gal, Aunt Sandra lived a rather lavish life of Southern values. She had a *sitting* room. Where people came to *sit!*

The beauty of her home always soothed me and inspired me to perfect the aesthetics of my own home.

The day before our departure for the two-hour drive south, my aunt's friend called to let us know that Aunt Sandra was in the hospital with pneumonia. So, we stopped at the hospital en route to Sandra's house to find a shriveled version of my six-foot-one, 83-year-old aunt. Having suffered with rheumatoid arthritis all her life, she had managed to camouflage the twisted body parts now prominent in the silhouette tangled in the sheets of the hospital bed. She was alert, though. She knew us and was fast to apologize for not greeting us with a cake, as all good Methodist women prepared for guests. This lapse in proper social etiquette seemed to disturb her more than her medical situation.

She didn't particularly look well, but she also didn't appear to be on death's door. We left her two hours later in search of sustenance, promising to return the next day.

Four a.m. Friday, February 21, 2020, the phone woke my parents and me. Sandra Lee Myers had passed in her sleep.

Two weeks later, the first confirmed case of COVID-19 was reported in Kanawha County, West Virginia's state capital. I know what you're thinking. I don't have an answer.

By mid-March, college and university spring breaks were lengthened, followed by a state mandate that all classes would finish the semester with virtual instruction. My son's much anticipated freshman year at WVU was cut short.

Not long after the state-wide closing of all public schools, my husband lost his job, putting us in the unemployment system with thousands of fellow Mountaineers. School children either rejoiced at the unexpected reprieve from the classroom or suffered through days without the security of that safe environment.

Americans glued themselves to the growing news of a widespread contagion covering our country. Businesses felt the sting of a declining economy. Hospitals were inundated with patients they didn't know how to treat. The shortage of hand sanitizer, antibacterial cleaners, and toilet paper led to consumer hoarding.

After the initial concern about my family's future, my survival instinct kicked in and I got busy. Instead of wallowing in self-pity and negativity, I decided to take advantage of the government request to stay home. I finished writing my next young adult novel. I spent every morning with my diary, posted on my blog, or visited the lives of my fictional characters. Writing has always calmed me, and there was no better time to seek solace.

When I wasn't writing, I knitted three baby blankets and learned I will probably *never* successfully knit a sock. By the first of May, I had exhausted my Netflix addiction and moved on to the Prime network. When I finally tired of the wastrel life, I decided to convert spare time into physical fitness. I exercised daily starting with a.m. stretches, midday Body Groove sessions, and evening physical therapy moves learned from previous sessions in the gym. Unfortunately, all of this self-love usually turned into a junk-food feeding frenzy, 'cause I "deserved it."

Social media became my best friend. Facebook offered a community of like-minded folks: MS Warriors, book geeks, writer friends, fellow parents, free knitting patterns, family, church services—it was all there. When Facebook didn't suffice, I learned about Instagram, Twitter, and Zoom (my nieces have already pointed out how technically behind I am).

Amazon online shopping gave me the instant gratification through the United States Postal Service that this Pandemic warrior needed. Who *doesn't* like getting packages in the mail? For three-plus months I enjoyed weekly deliveries right to my front door. At first my charge card bill was a concern; then I discovered the advantages of having Amazon Prime. I am now an Amazon junky. With my Prime membership I get free music downloads, access to movies, and purchase BONUSES that really add up.

The Pandemic (my very first and hopefully my last) also turned me in to a 21st century Gladys Kravitz, the iconic neighborhood snoop on the old *Bewitched* sitcom. I spent hours a day in my rocking chair gazing out at my lovely little neighborhood. I had a first row seat for rainstorms, suspicious foot travel, mail deliveries, and the Great 2020 Hydrangea Theft on McCue Avenue. My elderly neighbors across the street effortlessly cultivate seasonal flora. I love looking out at the assortment of color from my non-green thumb existence.

One early evening, I happened to glance outside the living room window to witness a young girl-child pull over on her bicycle, fling it to the ground, rush up to Ruth's front garden, and snatch a dark purple hydrangea before riding away with a glance over her shoulder. At first I smiled at the prank. Then she came back and grabbed two more blooms without even looking around for witnesses.

The audacity! Once was cute. Twice was criminal.

At this point, I was befuddled. What did I do? Open the front door and confront her? Report the crime to the neighbors? Alert the town cop of the incident? Not certain of flower-theft protocol, I did nothing; but I did keep a vigilant eye on further activity across the street.

If I felt helpless prior to Corona 2020, the lesson in self-preservation I received during this event reinforced in me an uncomfortable dependence. Already aware of my MS reality, the equation of COVID-19 plus Multiple Sclerosis left me paranoid, afraid, and anxious. For weeks, I clipped disease-monitoring newspaper articles for my daily journal. Then the local newspaper stopped going to print every day, revealing another scary truth. A shortage of cleaning supplies, toilet paper, bottled water, and paper towels ravaged the area while grocery aisles grew empty. Small business owners went bankrupt while alcohol consumption grew. I wasn't totally convinced this wasn't the Biblically-promised Apocalypse.

By July, the fate of schools resuming in the fall was unresolved. Sporting events across the nation were cancelled. Positive cases of COVID-19 spiked once again. The world as we once knew it had become a masked society.

What were we to do? In the words of children's author Michael Rosen, "We can't go over it. We can't go under it. Oh no! We've got to go through it!" (*We're Going on a Bear Hunt*, 1989). That's what we Americans do. We work through it.

It looks like I have more time to work on that knitted sock.

(Previously published in *A New Normal: Voices From A Pandemic*, Headline Books, 2020)

Lisa McComb's Young Adult fiction is the recipient of both national and international acclaim. As a retired public educator, she continues to utilize the expertise of former students in the creation of characters for her Church of Go *series.* I Have MS. What's Your Super Power? *is Lisa's commonsense guide to living with multiple sclerosis.*

Vacation Joy

Eldon Winston – Martinsburg, West Virginia, USA

I awake late with no events scheduled
  just me and my projects.
Breakfast finally done, I start on the closet
  cleaning, repairing and painting.
The sun sets before I do much.
Check emails after supper, then bed.

Sunshine lights the bedroom, telling me
  a hot day's made for mowing.
Meals are unhurried with no place to go.
The day comes to go to town for food and
  oil for the riding mower.
Masks ready my wife and I go for groceries.
We are counted in.
We emerge with next week's menu in bags.
Stop at the auto parts store and home we go.

I work on the closet after our naps.
Avoiding COVID-19 I use my digital RIFE machine
  for any COVID-19 virus I might have.
My wife ignores my health projects but she also
  washes hands and socially distances.
We are in no hurry.

Eldon Winston says: *"Writing for fun has been one of my hobbies for decades. When I was younger, I'd practice the craft after I got home from work or school, but now I'm just trying to express my views to the world. Not too bad for an Industrial Psychologist."*

Guardian Angels on Motorbikes (fiction)

Catherine Harris – Cape Town, Western Cape, South Africa

"You'll be arrested as soon as you try to cross the provincial border."

Desperation and anger rose in my throat as I faced this supercilious young police officer at the third station I had tried. Each attempt received the same indifferent response.

"But my mother is ill. See, I have a doctor's letter. She is elderly and living on her own. I need to be with her." I hated my vulnerability and felt burning hot tears despite my best attempt to retain control.

"The rules are clear. No interprovincial travelling unless you have a death certificate."

"So, my mother has to die before I get to see her?"

Back home, I replayed this conversation over and over in my mind. What could I do? All main routes out of town had permanent roadblocks, and my landscaping business was not deemed "essential," so I didn't have a travel permit. As I stood in my kitchen looking into my back garden, I watched the gardener, Brightly, sweeping up leaves. His being there was illegal, but he had a family back in Malawi to support and had pleaded with me to allow him to continue working.

Brightly reliably arrived once a week on his trusty blue Yamaha motorbike, which was parked round the back, out of sight. Times were tough for everyone at the moment—we were all trying to make it work, and this meant occasionally bending the rules. A small seed of an idea started to form.

If I drove the back roads, I could get close to the border. The only way over by car would encounter roadblocks. However, if I could travel off-road, using hiking tracks and farm roads, I could get to my mother's house relatively easily. She lived alone, about twenty kilometres from the border, in a small rural town. I mulled this over before walking outside with a mug of tea for Brightly.

"How would you like to earn some extra money?" was my opening gambit. I felt guilty already for what I was going to propose, knowing it was unlikely Brightly would be able to turn me down. He had a wife and children living back home and was already working illegally here before the lockdown. Like many others, Brightly existed on the fringes of society, trying to keep a low profile while desperately trying to make a living and a better life for himself and his family. He had worked for me for two years, and while I knew a bit about him, I made a conscious effort not to get too involved. I told myself that maintaining a professional distance was for the best. After all, I was Brightly's employer, not his friend.

Now I was about to cross that line to suit my own needs.

I outlined my plan, making light of the dangers and emphasising the cash payment I was prepared to make.

"Yes, Mami, it's no problem." He beamed.

"So we would need to leave later today. Do you need to go home and fetch anything?"

"No, Mami. I have everything here," he said, indicating his small backpack.

I quickly made last-minute preparations. I packed a small backpack of my own with essentials—money, water and snacks, some clothes, basic medical supplies, and a head torch, and ensured my cell phone was fully charged. I pored over a map, trying to remember old hiking routes, memorising them, but tore the page out just in case.

By late afternoon, we had loaded Brightly's motorbike into the back of my bakkie, securing it as best we could. Before climbing in, I handed Brightly a crisp wad of notes drawn from the ATM that afternoon. I had a last-minute attack of guilt and nerves.

"Are you sure you're okay helping me? This is dangerous. If we are stopped . . . . " I left the sentence hanging.

"It's no problem, Mami." He smiled confidently at me, seemingly unconcerned at the journey we were about to undertake—but then, his life experience had been vastly different from mine.

I calculated we had three hours of decent light left, the first two of which would be on reasonable roads. Brightly sat in awkward silence up front with me in the cab. I turned on the radio to break the void while trying to concentrate on what lay ahead. We made good time despite using the more circuitous backroads, and traffic was minimal. The last hour before the light faded was hard. We followed rough dirt roads, climbed slightly into the foothills, and skirted farmhouses and isolated hamlets. Traveling parallel to the main highway, we occasionally caught glimpses of it from our elevated position. We passed a few people, mostly workers walking or cycling home at the end of the day. All watched us curiously, taking in the white woman driving with her male companion sitting up front. My company name was clearly visible down the sides and my plates weren't local. Not much I could do about that. I held my breath every time I saw another car approaching, but we continued without any mishaps. Brightly remained quietly stoic beside me.

Light diminished as we reached a narrow valley, and the track petered out. I pulled off the road, bumping over a rocky field into a thicket, and parked behind some trees. I climbed out to check that my bakkie would not be immediately visible to casual passersby.

We offloaded the motorbike. I pointed out the winding hiking path we needed to follow. I could see my breath as the temperature had dropped and the last light of day became a faint smear behind us on the far horizon.

Brightly kick-started the bike, the sound of the engine seeming to amplify and reverberate off the dark valley walls. I awkwardly climbed on, my pack making me feel ungainly. It seemed too late to question the sanity of this journey now. I was committed.

"We go?" Brightly asked. Without waiting on my response, he drove off, jolting and bumping down the path, leaving me no option but to grab and hold him tightly around his waist. His jacket smelt of wood smoke and soap. I was aware this was all surreal and would've been unthinkable pre-lockdown. But this was not a time for being socially sensitive. I needed to remain focussed on potential obstacles and danger ahead of us. This next section would be the real test, and I was praying my memory was accurate.

In the dark, we approached the river crossing, and I was counting on the ford still being there. I could smell the river and the damp earth. The motorbike lights were not very strong, and our approach down the steep track was too fast. Before we knew it, the bike ploughed into a thick, waterlogged reed bank, wheels spinning up mud. After some hard work, we managed to extricate the bike, and Brightly extended his hand to pull me up the bank. We backtracked, attempting to cross further up beneath low trees and thick vegetation.

"Careful, Mami!" Brightly warned me. I quickly ducked, managing to miss a low branch that would have whipped me off the bike. Stopping for a moment, he turned round to see if I were okay, then nodded silently before continuing across a rocky fording point. Icy water seeped into my shoes before we climbed up the other side.

We made slow progress along a narrow path that wound up to a ridge. There were no lights up there—we were truly on our own. At the top, we could see down into the valley floor below and the lights of the small town where my mother lived. Over an hour later, making tedious progress, we made it to a small, tarred road.

The relief at finally seeing my mother was overwhelming. She sat wrapped up warmly in her armchair, her slender frailty, lined face, and shrunken stature a visible reminder of her recent battle.

"My word, how on earth did you get here?" she asked.

"I'm very fortunate to have a skilled cross-country driver who made sure I made it to you in one piece. I am forever indebted to him for getting me here," I said, my voice wobbling a bit as the magnitude of it all began to sink in.

I introduced Brightly, who clearly felt out of place and embarrassed at all the fuss. I wondered how my elderly mother would react to having a strange Malawian man standing in her living room at this time of night. She didn't miss a beat.

"Some of us never get to meet our guardian angels, but I am so glad I get to meet yours. Now I can thank him personally for getting you safely to me. Would you be a dear and make us all a cup of tea? I think we need it."

Catherine Harris is a Freight Forwarder by day, writer by night, mother to two teenagers, and an unfit, sporadic mountain runner. She lives in Cape Town, South Africa, and cannot wait to see the big-sky open space of the Karoo again once lockdown ends.

Awkward

Meg Whitlatch – Mendoza, Argentina

Awkward. That's the only word that can describe the way I felt. We were out for the allowed evening stroll when I saw two familiar faces—Nico and Juan, twin brothers who'd been my students some years ago. What a joy to run into someone amid the quarantine restrictions! I almost forgot the rules.

Normally we would have embraced in a hug and kissed on our cheeks. I would have asked about their lives and patted their backs. We would've hugged and greeted again before parting. They were dear students, and I had shared five years of high school with them.

But this time was different—it was weird, felt unnatural. We lifted our elbows and bumped them from a distance. Our face masks covered our huge smiles of happiness for seeing each other, and then we left, just like that, without any kind of hug or greeting.

Meg Whitlatch is a teacher and interpreter living in Mendoza, Argentina.

Coversion

John R Yost – Martinsburg, West Virginia, USA

A disease spawns a disguise.
Who would think that COVID
would so quickly go covert.
Gone are days when masks
are donned for Hallowe'en,
surgery, dust protection,
or convenience store robberies.
Acquaintances pass unrecognized,
when known hold their breath
and maintain appropriate remoteness.
No need to mask facial expressions
with clever facades to cloak feelings.
Layered fabric conceals all,
a disguise suitable for every occasion.

John R Yost lives in Martinsburg, West Virginia. His poetry has previously been published in Pivot, Appalachian Review, *and* Anthology of Appalachian Writers – Karen Spears Zacharias Volume XI.

The Corona

Rodica Todd – Seaford, East Sussex, United Kingdom

It's Thursday, eight o'clock. The sound of applause for the National Health Service is more and more forceful. People come out on doorsteps, clapping until their palms get red and tired.

Sometimes I miss the clap because I'm working in shifts, three consecutive, twelve-hour days—hidden in my PPE—followed by another two at home to rest physically, mostly mentally. It's difficult to relieve stress when nine out of ten patients have just passed away.

Then the news helps me sum up the winnings. This is when I start crying. Depending on results, there is little, very little, chance for joy. I am a good doctor but not a merciful God.

The people in the intensive care unit share a terrifying experience. I scan every patient. On each bed there's another ME, a preview of what the future could hold for any of us. Then I ask myself, "Will I catch the virus and die like Sonia?" She was only thirty-five, caring, devoted to her job, full of life.

When nothing can be done anymore, we give the body "some dignity"—we take all the tubes out, waiting for Peace to kick in. It is too late for goodbyes. There's a little girl still waiting to say, "Hello, Daddy," who, just like Bambi, cannot make sense of such events. What is dignity, after all? I did my research, and I came across these synonyms: nobility, majesty, regality. Shall I tell a ten-year-old that her dad departed like a king? Too many kings have lost such a battle.

On the sofa, with cat and dogs close by, I dare shut my eyes for a while. I can see through Corona's round shape covered in spikes, clinging onto every lung cell. Like a ghost, it reaches the inside of my chest and locks itself in. There it gets mad, out of control, and stops me from breathing in any possible way. I am its victim. Shall I take off the mask? There are throbbing lines on my face.

We hear that "most people infected with COVID-19 will undergo mild to moderate symptoms and recover without requiring special treatment." But what if you are old? What if you suffer from heart disease, diabetes, cancer, or asthma?

In the intensive care we look at each other helplessly, then appoint the one condemned to afterlife. Who will go first? "It might be you, second bed at the window, you who are overweight. Or maybe you, who are short of breath, or you who had a heart attack. You, you, not you—you're too young to die."

We label the old as frail and vulnerable. Bordered by wrinkles, with shaky hands, some in wheelchairs, some with walking sticks, some already forgotten, some losing their identity, *all* there, in the shadows of a home, following the same pattern. Patterns exist since the dawn of time, making it easy to generalise. Nevertheless, Corona surprises us with what we call "its model of asymptomatic nature"—which means we are able to predict neither its preferences nor its next move.

Corona is the eye opener. In self-isolation we learned to read its message: there is no pattern for pain, sorrow, sufferance, as each of us is unique. We hurt differently—but no matter the age, we do hurt *a lot*.

Corona makes me think of the crown of thorns worn by Jesus on his way to crucifixion, belittled by the mob. Corona is our punishment. We forget God. *We* are God now, the ones who *must* decide whether a ventilator goes to an over-65 or to the 40-year-old. Age is irrelevant. How can we judge fairly? The older is as precious as the younger. The poor might be a better person than the rich. Surely, a good soul deserves a second chance.

There, on the sofa, I drop off, feeling the spikes of Corona in my soul, deep, dark, suffocating me with guilt. I keep on repeating it to myself: "I am the doctor, *not* God." Then I dream . . . .

A dream to come true:

When that daylight will appear
We'll get rid of our fear,
Rid of 'thorns' on Earth's sphere.

We *will* celebrate in style,
Lock Corona in its file.

All my children will be here,
We will wipe each others' tear,

Go with hora round the world,
Hold the hand with young and old.
Love and laugh and also play,
Breathe!
Corona ran away.

Swallows attack the Virus. They pluck out its 'spikes' to ease the deadly menace on mankind. They might be the same ones who flew and pulled out the thorns of Golgotha to balance Good and Evil.

Swallows say "hello" to every new day with a stretch of wing and a happy song. They have been considered sacred since they removed the thorns from Jesus's forehead when crucified. They are the ones who will rid *us* of the thorns of Corona—pain, sorrow and death.

Original art by Rodica Todd
(Watercolour on cardboard, 40.5 cm x 30.5 cm)

Rodica Todd *of Seaford, United Kingdom, says, "Writing about COVID-19 is like juggling with Misfortune and Fortune at the same time. When the whole world seems to crumble, there are ways to bring it together again: by sharing love and positivity."*

Dry

Courtney Susman – Lewisburg, West Virginia, USA

Give me three random items on a good day:
Let's say a blue ribbon,
a pale damask sheet,
and a bamboo bowl.

I would meld those pieces into a canopy
to shield me from the sun or light droplets.
It would tie nicely to the magnolia tree,
in front of my apartment.

Using the blue ribbon,
I could also attach the same sheet-covered bowl
to the plant hook on my living room ceiling,
and fly a kite inside when it's raining.

Now the bowl a sieve,
the sheet a rushing river in a treacherous territory,
the ribbon flecks of gold;
I summon the chilly water by dipping my hand in the fabric.

On a good day, give me three random items,
and I transport myself from home.
Now I look at three random objects and wonder,
How can I make those into a mask?

I grab my bamboo bowl,
replace its contents:
two apples, a peach, an orange,
with sewing supplies.

The CDC says 100% cotton.
I dig up my pale damask sheet;

it's low on the rotation.
I follow an approved pattern.

I listen well.
Without a machine,
it takes eight hours.
My mask has a crooked body.

I cut the blue ribbon
used to cinch my curtains
and attach the pieces.
Now it has limbs.

Items are now intentional.
Good days have been dry.
My imagination is practical;
it transports me nowhere.

Courtney Susman *received her MFA in Theatre Performance from The University of Southern Mississippi and BFA in theatre from Marshall University. In addition to directing and performing, she has taught theatre and humanities at Marshall University, The University of Southern Mississippi, and New River Community Technical College. She is a member of Actors' Equity Association.*

A Fresh Start

Davion Moore – Sandusky, Ohio, USA

When I first heard about the stay-at-home order, I imagine I had the same response as so many others.

"What? A stay-at-home order?"

I can picture the initial confusion on my face. Then again, I probably kept my composure—at least to the best of my ability—as it is something I have mastered over the years. But even for a (Jedi?) master like myself, this unfamiliar term was difficult to process.

Now, let me start off by saying that yes, I am a homebody. I would much rather be reading the likes of Baldwin, Hemingway, and other literary giants whose works live on my shelf than being out with a crowd of people. However, this felt different. The lives and careers of my grandparents, who love to be outdoors, and my mother, who works within the hospital, will be impacted as well. That's when it hit me: maybe this illness is more severe than I thought.

The stay-at-home order for Ohio went into effect on March 23 at 11:59 p.m. The day before, I went to the store with my aunt, and I was intrigued by what I saw—empty shelves and tons of people rushing to get food, hand sanitizer, and other items in preparation for the upcoming lockdown. As we sped through the aisles, more and more people grabbed whatever they could. And it made me realize something. We were all scared. We were all confused. We were entirely unsure of what lay ahead. The world as we knew it was about to change. As I walked through the store with my mask, the atmosphere felt gloomy. It was a strange feeling, and something I'm not sure will ever be replicated.

As my aunt and I left the store, our family prepared for the upcoming change. We went through our regular routine of watching movies, playing board games, and spending time with one another. When I returned to my place, I once again tried to make sense of the stay-at-home order. I wanted to piece together what was going on, but it didn't make sense. And as I went to bed, I still could not fathom it. Late nights are when I do my best thinking, and I used the entire night to think about it—but still nothing, no understanding. Then, when it was time to get my day started, I went through my normal daily routine. My day consists of school work, writing, and spending time with family. I did just that before 11:59 hit, and then the lockdown became a reality.

When the lockdown started, the very first thing I did was grab a canvas. My brother had an old pack of canvases that he'd left at my place. By no means am I a painter. My brother is the artist of the family and has done incredible work, including paintings, animation, and much more. I also have not painted in at least eight years. Regardless, I grabbed a canvas, paints, and newspaper (to avoid an inevitable mess), and started to paint.

I realized that during this odd time, we needed all the positivity we could get. I painted inspiring items such as a sunny day, an inspirational quote, flowers (that still need to be finished), and clouds that formed words such as "hope" and "peace." Are they masterpieces? Not at all. But they were therapeutic. It was a way to challenge myself and get out of my comfort zone. It was something that needed to be done.

As time went on, I decided to try other things. I kept a poetry journal, read about/started a new hobby in gardening, and became fascinated with reiki, meditation, and Tai Chi. I managed to stay busy, all while doing things to stay "fit" mentally. A difficult time such as this one can be mentally exhausting and drains you as you try to maneuver it. Painting, as well as the other activities, were a way to "escape," and I enjoyed every minute. It did not hurt that most of them were things I wanted to try anyway, but a hectic school schedule kept me from pursuing them. What better time to try these activities than now? Personally, I can't think of one.

The current state of the world is quite strange and scary. It's important to keep ourselves and our families as healthy as possible. However, I don't mean physically. While physical health is a huge aspect of surviving these times, the health I am referring to is mental health. Use this time to analyze your life choices, unwind, and remind yourself that dark times never last. Ask yourself, "Are you happy with your life?" If not, what choices can you make to improve your situation? Is it an easy thing to do? Not at all. But it's worthwhile.

Do what makes you happy and/or what keeps you calm—especially if it's something new. Appreciate the small things in life like a sunset, time with your loved ones, or even birds chirping outside your window. Cherish them and live in the moment as they occur. It's one of the best things you can do.

Davion Moore is a lifelong writer who recently gained the confidence to share his words with the world. He's an Ohio native who loves writing, reading, and watching sports. Davion has degrees in Financial Management and Economics, and hopes to pursue a Master's in Creative Writing.

Life Has Changed

Nonceba Sogcwayi (15 years old) – Benoni, Gauteng, South Africa

Life has changed! Our lives have taken a U-turn in the middle of nowhere.

Life is full of surprises, but 2020 brought us the biggest surprise of our lives. We never expected our world would stop due to a sickness/disease entering the doors of the world without even knocking or giving us a chance to prepare for what was coming.

We are still adjusting to the fact that our lives have to depend on wearing masks, sanitising everywhere we go and as often as possible, and keeping a 1.5m distance in public places.

Imagine not being able to see a friend or loved one for months—and when you do finally get that opportunity, you can't even give them a warm, loving hug.

How cruel can the world be? This makes me think of prison. In prisons, you are not supposed to hug a visitor, no matter how much you have missed them. Some take that risk because they just can't hold themselves back, but they know doing so might even cost an individual his/her life.

We have lost the way we used to live our lives, but most of all we have lost our loved ones, which is not an easy journey to take. There are other families who have to bury two or three members at once. I know of neighbours who received the message their father passed on—while they were at the graveyard burying their daughter—and their mother was in quarantine and couldn't be there.

The hardest thing about what we're experiencing is that we can get infected and our bodies may not show any signs— which can mean we infect others without even knowing we're risking our families' lives.

No matter how scared we are of dying from this pandemic, we really don't want to risk another person's life, so it's good to isolate either at home or at a quarantine hospital. It won't be easy staying away from our parents, kids, or even partner, but it's for everybody's safety. Just remember, it's all about safety first.

SCHOOL! SCHOOL! SCHOOL! I never in my life really thought I'd miss school the way I do now, but seriously, I really do miss learning. I remember talking to a friend who doesn't like school even a bit, but since we started quarantine, she was the first to text me and say she really misses school. I never expected such from her, but it's been months since we've been to school. I even miss sitting on a desk and listening to the teacher.

I really am looking forward to going back to school, even though I know it won't be the same as it was before we had corona in our country. We won't be able to hug our friends anymore, hold hands like we used to, or sit in groups to just laugh and listen to each other talking. I guess we have to accept this situation. IT IS WHAT IT IS.

A lot of parents have lost their jobs because of the pandemic. The economy is bad, and it will take time for it to be normal again.

Some people have not taken this pandemic seriously, which is sad. People are dying from COVID-19, but they still are not taking precautionary measures by wearing a mask. If you don't have a mask, at least find a scarf to cover your nose and mouth to protect yourself and others.

Masks are really not comfortable, but we still need to wear them for our own safety and for the safety of people around us. Not everything is about you—it's also about the people around you too. Nothing in life stays forever.

We are a nation—we are one. We should do whatever it takes to keep each other safe.

I know it's not your responsibility to take care of other people, but if others are doing it for you, why can't you do it for them?

BE SAFE AND EVERYONE WILL BE SAFE.

Nonceba Sogcwayi *is a fifteen-year-old girl who loves reading, writing and listening to motivational messages. She likes giving advice to people and encouraging them to do better or try to be the best they can be. She works hard and gives her best in everything she does.*

The Dearth

Filjoh – Vancouver, Washington, USA

All this time yet all this dearth of poem in my pen!
Like no wind upon my ocean,
salt water all around and not a drop for me to drink,
all this expanse of air but it breathes like mud,
because, they say, of the invisible bug.

I've been left like a tide without a pool,
a toad without a stool,
even bored enough to drool.
Now's no time for a masterpiece—any words will have to do
if that's what it takes to unloosen my screw.
O my Muse, why did you run and hide?
Were I to choose, I would have up and died!
Yes, I've enjoyed reading dear Rossetti,
but now my rhyme sounds like confetti.
I admit it is better to read than write sometimes,
but this is grim: what rhymes with 'COVID-19?'

Let me see . . . 'COVID-19' backwards, yes it be, is '911-VOC'
and that makes a pair with 'Great Depression-2020'
which leads on to 'Famine-21' of course
then it's 'who-oh-who-can-save-us-in-22,'
and once I stop crying,
we can follow on with 'World War-23'
then 'sorry-for-you-if-you're-still-alive-by-25'
because the brave New digital World Order will dominate by
    28,
and The Great Reboot will be *finie* on Sunday three, 2033.
I get it: 'COVID' rhymes this decade in its entirety!

It all looks like blood and Gore from here,
and bucks galore for the bluescreen whores.

I sit and I watch, and I wait some more,
but why do I Zoom, for what reason?
To say a heterodox word has become a treason:
it's staring into these Windows that is so displeasin'!
You say I need a mask to wear to enter through the BillGates
of Hell?
I'll make mine a char-black dragon snout
with flames of spiky red dots spraying out!

Filjoh *is a hazmat trucker whose pastimes include writing, esoteric studies, art collecting, and transiting through life's greatest challenges, renewed.*

Fresca and My Garage

Vicki Crawford – Scott Depot, West Virginia, USA

My daughter and her boyfriend hesitated to visit me because COVID-19 had already hit Boston, where they lived. We decided to risk it, and they arrived the day before my birthday. They intended to stay one week, but then the quarantine began. They remained for almost three months. Our new normal consisted of them using my home office and working remotely. I worked on my new garage workbench, with the garage door open. It was like an outdoor office.

The birds flew by outside the garage door. My oscillating fan blasted cool air when the days grew too hot. Neighbors walked by with their dogs. Neighborhood children each brought their own basketballs, but kept using one another's when one was free. Epic failure! I heard one of them proclaim, "I am the king. You should call me that." A girl responded, "I am not calling you the king." Then they debated over whether cheerleaders were athletes and decided a cheerleader did nothing to merit that title.

The oscillating fan whirred as I texted Stacy, my hair stylist and friend. I told her I needed to dye my hair soon—which I hadn't done since the 1990s. I learned to line the kitchen sink with garbage bags so the hair dye wouldn't stain it. I watched YouTube videos on how to do it. Stacy laughed via text. I worry the pandemic will cause her to lose the shop. Not for myself, but for her and her family. It's how they earn their living.

I missed hugs from friends. If I went out to the stores, I couldn't even hug my daughter. That was hard! There were people I hugged each week, and to lose that was a huge loss. I felt the void from that one simple gesture! I may have even cried at the loss of hugs because they make me feel comforted. Human.

The garage was my sanctuary. It took four years to redo. I had help along the way. Most notably, from my friend Mike.

If not for his help, I'd still be knee-deep in boxes of papers and unable to lift all the heavy items. He helped me transform it into an amazing workspace for myself. There are friends who are valuable, but some are invaluable. As I admire my pegboard wall, which I do all the time, I see the pegboards holding various tapes. I organize it even more. *Painters tape. Carpet tape. Masking tape. Electrical tape. Duct tape. Double sided tape. Scotch tape.* I straighten the screwdrivers. I have an old comic book on my pegboard wall. It has traveled all over the garage during reno and it sort of belongs there. I couldn't think of a better home for it once the garage was finished. As I admire my pegboard wall again, I roll up the extension cords—and then crack a nail.

I sigh heavily and search YouTube videos for how to remove acrylic nails. I soak them in acetone and wrap them in foil papers. It takes hours to remove them all. I am terrible at it. My nails are brittle, so I put on fake nails. I sit at the dining room table painting nail polish on fake nails I ordered online in a variety of colors. I buy nail glue—not the kind from the hardware store, but the kind for fingernails. They last about two weeks. I am stirring spaghetti sauce and see one is missing. I search the house to find it before I throw out the sauce. I later find it on the floor of the laundry room.

I think about the staff at the nail salon and worry they will lose their business too. Then I begin to think—when did I get so incompetent? There was a day I could do my own hair and nails! How did I get to be so pampered? It was only a couple of years ago I started getting my hair flat ironed at the salon because I was terrible at it. Then around the same time, I began getting my nails done at a salon for the first time in my life. I had neglected those things due to all the home improvement I had going on around our home.

One day I decided I deserved to take care of myself. I deserved to get my nails done. I deserved to do a lot of things. So, I refuse to feel guilty for self-care. I refuse to feel badly for pampering myself for a change. I put on makeup to go out. My daughter asked, "Why are you so dressed up?"

I laughed. "I rarely get to go out during this pandemic, so I'm going to look good doing it." So, there I was dressed for success to go to the Post Office. And happy to do so!

The biggest mission I had did not involve antibacterial wipes or toilet paper, because luckily I buy both in bulk and had enough prior to the pandemic. My problem? I could no longer find many of my necessities—which aren't the same as everyone else's. I'm talking about low sodium ham, edamame for salads, brown sugar bacon, and Fresca. Yes, Fresca. I need my Fresca. I searched everywhere in our town, but to no avail. I'm fairly sure the nice young woman I kept asking at the grocery was tired of my endless quest for Fresca, but you never miss what you have until it's gone. I didn't know how much I needed it.

At one point, I went to get tested for COVID-19 during the free tests in our town. Having a gigantic swab stuck up your nose into your brain was a shock. It smarted! But worth it. I did not have COVID-19. I had allergies. I kept watching the news, reading blogs and stories that were of a serious nature about the pandemic, and surely it was that. I was thankful my daughter was with me instead of being in Boston.

However, I also subscribe to the school of thought that if I begin to let fear overwhelm me, I will never be able to live. I have multiple sclerosis. The dark side of that autoimmune condition is loss of mobility, eyesight, hearing, speaking—any number of challenging things. The medication I take for it enables me to function as well as I do—yet it also can cause a brain infection that can kill me. There is a dark side to all medical conditions, but if I allow my brain to go there, I would have wasted years of my life being in fear instead of living my life.

I never pretend it isn't serious, but I don't allow myself to feel that negativity. I don't allow it to control me because I am still in control. Come the day I'm not in control, it will be different. To me, the same goes for the pandemic. It is serious, it is awful, it is frightening. However, I won't dwell on all the things that could go wrong. I see a lot of my friends doing that. I'm taking precautions as we all should be, and quarantining when I need to do so, and trying my best not to be negative or scared.

To those who live in fear, I wish them to remember life is not about the fear of death. It is about living. Is that hard to do during a pandemic? Yes! But still, try to focus on living. Appreciate moments. Realize the significance of this one horrible thing that has connected the entire world. Taught us what truly matters. But remember the good in life. The funny. The sweet. The ridiculous, even.

I did my own hair, I did my own nails, and I looked good enough. Still competent. I have my amazing daughter. I have a bucket of different masks on a shelf in the kitchen. I have masks in my car. I have masks in my purse. I have masks to match every outfit. I have knock-off brands of antibacterial wipes and a stack of toilet paper. And my garage sanctuary— I have that! What I still don't have is Fresca.

Vicki Crawford's *writing has appeared in* Anthology of Appalachian Writers, Crystal Wilkinson Volume XII, Anthology of Appalachian Writers, Wiley Cash Volume X, Diner Stories: Off the Menu *and* Appalachian Heritage. *She has received many award for her writings, including a Denny C. Plattner Honorable Mention for Outstanding Fiction of the Year from Appalachian Heritage.*

Apart—Together

Michael – Graaff Reinet, Eastern Cape, South Africa

Think about that!
Stay home – stay safe
Home is the new prison
The prison of fear
Lock up the minds
Do as you're told
Cover your faces
Your identity's stolen
Stay and obey
Don't question or think
Your opinion is a crime
Name and shame
No contact. No talking
Do as you're told
It's for your own good!
You have been told
Your freedom is sold.

Michael lives in the most beautiful place on earth, Graaff Reinet, the plains of the Karoo. He gets most of his inspiration from the people and the landscape. He's an avid reader and loves cats.

Collection of Various Idiosyncratic Deliberations

Dolores Porretta-Brown – Sunderland, Tyne and Ware,
United Kingdom

**Collection Of Various Idiosyncratic Deliberations
Containing Overall Valued Individual Decisions**

You may have heard about or even seen the film *A Room With A View*. We are very lucky to have a wonderful view, especially recently. Recently? Yes, indeed. Recently—or is it the new now? Bizarre, weird, surreal—all words that have sprung to mind when trying to describe the world we suddenly find ourselves in.

We live in a flat often referred to as a box with one wall all glass, which looks out onto the open sea and harbour. While I should be retired, I still work—when there is any. I live with my other half, John, who is retired. One of the many reasons I put up with him—apart from loving him—is that he does put up with me, no mean task! He is older, though thankfully fit, while I, suffering CFS (Chronic Fatigue Syndrome) with no immune system, have had to isolate—which means he has as well—not easy. I could ramble on about all the activities we've had to forgo, but so has everyone. Instead, I endeavour to be positive and look at a half glass full, especially when it's red wine. We **Can Overcome Vicious Insidious Disease.**

So what have these past months been like? As I said, we live opposite the sea, a beautiful open space. We have not had young children to entertain all day and not lived in fear of losing our jobs—all good so far. Apart from missing freedom, the main thing many we know have missed are their family and, being in a certain age bracket, their grandchildren. They say what you never have, you never miss, so not having much family left and no grandchildren, we have not missed them. You have to remain positive, especially if you wish to survive.

We all know life **Can Often Vary In Direction,** so one has to adapt or go under. First adaption for us was online shopping. Being registered as vulnerable, one supermarket contacted me offering deliveries—brilliant. Actually, setting it up was another story, taking two weeks, but eventually it was resolved. A second store backed up with provisions, so nourishment was sorted, especially the alcohol situation, a reason I feel for many thinking their clothes have shrunk! So we **Continue Onwards Vigilant In Determination.**

Online shopping has been a source of amusement and on-going activity. One would think it should take less time than having to go out to a shop. Wrong! First up you have to book a 'slot,' then order a minimum amount of food to secure it. Nearer the delivery time, you find you need other items, so it's online again. Then just before delivery, the substitution list comes up. Love it. 'We are sorry that some items you have ordered are not available, so we have substituted them with the following.' Had a few interesting substitutions, but my favourite so far was when I ordered an emergency dental filling kit for the first filling that dropped out. It was replaced with—guess what?—no, not polyfiller, but dental floss! Still trying to work that one out. Even better, when relating this to a friend, she knew of someone who ordered Tenas [adult diapers] and was sent a packet of baps [soft, white buns]! I was unaware of what Tena's were, so John had to explain it to me, since he watches more TV than me. Many ladies will concur—adverts are usually when you get up to do that little job, whether it's checking on how the washing is getting on or turning up the oven.

Conversant On Vast Incessant Duties, ladies? Must say I am not a feminist—I just believe in equality and fair division of labour for all. To qualify my ignorance about Tenas, I often refer to myself as a camel—not because of any hump, I hasten to add, but because my main 'toiletries' are morning and evening. When out, I only visit the ladies' room to check on its décor, believing a lot can be ascertained about an establishment by the quality of the toilets.

Let's **Concentrate On Valuable Interesting Decisions.** One of the first decisions I made was to get some sort of routine going to give each day a purpose. It felt sensible to partake in some sort of past normality, for 'normality' as we knew it, if not gone forever, will be a long time in returning. I always said the only way our flat would be tidy would be if I were locked in it for three months. Well, I think John wrote a letter! So various hours each day were allocated to tidying. I'm not sure how charity shops will cope when they re-open.

My accountant recommends keeping accounts for seven years instead of five, but as my father's daughter, I was well trained in keeping all accounts for ten years, just to be sure. However, when I came across visas dating back to 1992, even I thought that was excessive. We must have filled nearly ten blue refuse bins, and still files and files remain. Where did all those boxes of photo albums come from? As we are often told, a clear space makes for a clear mind; a tidy area makes for a tidy life. Not sure if that's exactly the life I aim for, but it's satisfying to clear unused items OUT.

Clearing Out Valueless Items Declutters life. Technology, while I don't know what many would have done without it recently, is not my favourite thing. I am not a dedicated follower of social media. It takes all my time to answer essential e-mails, so if I started scrolling, my day would quickly pass. However, one decision I did make as part of my new routine was to post a thought every day on the dreaded Facebook. I say dreaded, as generally I only use it to remind me of birthdays—and to contact people whose number I may not have.

One Monday was Anne Frank's birthday, so I dedicated the week to her bravery, creativeness, and inspiration. Here we are bemoaning the fact we're practically prisoners in our own homes, while she, along with seven others, was incarcerated in an attic for two years.

She wrote, "The nicest part is being able to write down (all?) my thoughts and feelings. Otherwise, I might suffocate." I empathize with that. She, as you know, left an incredible account of life during her unimaginable existence, and some truly inspirational thoughts. What a girl! "Where there's hope, there's life." "An empty day, though clear and bright, is just as dark as any night." "Those who are happy will make others happy," and numerous other quotes.

Thinking about happiness, spreading happiness, and how lucky I am to have a friend such as the mate I had coffee with today, brought a smile to my face. Just think about any friend you consider yourself lucky enough to know, and that will bring a smile. Bet you can think of more than one!

Be certain that you **Can Obtain Victory In Defiance**—it just takes effort. I do believe that if you keep telling yourself something long enough, it has a better chance of happening as opposed to giving up at the first hurdle. Every dog has its day—just some dogs have to wait longer than others. Whatever you go through in life, look for any bonus it could bring, not at what has been taken away. I've always thought a big kick up the posterior makes you address life in a different way. Otherwise, one just trundles on in the same old way and eventually goes under. CVF was certainly my big kick, and while there any many things I miss greatly, I accept they have gone, enjoyed them while I could, but now my life is different. But I still have a life, and so do any of you who are reading this. It may not be as you would wish, but don't concentrate on that—unless you wish to remain miserable (because I admit it is easy to be drawn down that path). Search for the positive and put your thinking cap on as how to cope with it.

So, in **Conclusion, Obliterate Vacuous Indecisive Doubts**. "I don't think of all the misery but of the beauty that still remains" and "Think of all the beauty still left around you and be happy."—Anne Frank.

Dolores Porretta-Brown *is a freelance actor/director mainly in live performance; designer, dramaturg, and critic. Observer of life while very active in it.*

Trick or Treat

Chip Ferrell – Parkersburg, West Virginia, USA

Photograph by Chip Ferrell

Even Princess Anna (Amelia Ferrell, age 3) must maintain social distancing during Trick or Treat. A three-foot grabber helps handover the goods without breaching protocol.

Virus Versus Us

Mark Lyndon – Swansea, Wales, United Kingdom

An intangible, inaudible enemy invisibly invades.

Insidious seems an anthropomorphic germ's encroachment.

Virulence defines this incipient virus.

An anathematic pathogen revels in hellish bedevilment.

Anagrammatically vile, evil; heinousness is her sinister
essence.

Forever far from philanthropic looks a microscopic,
misanthropic speck.

Ever-clever, under cover, the disingenuous genius deviously
cleaves our armour with ardour.

Immorally seeking immortality, she possesses a sneaking
proclivity for proximity, and plans heists on hosts.

Meanwhile, ill-fated all quail.

We feel enfeebled, afeared afore adversity, an atavistic
adversary.

Dignity appears robbed when vindictive iniquity
surreptitiously steals unseen.

Impending gloom looms; primes dim doom's grim time-
bomb.

Malign pneumonia perniciously attacks, wracks, wrecks,
wreaks chaos.

What a demonic pandemic!

Pandemonium emanates from ravaged, savaged lungs which
gasp; grasping nebulous nothingness.

Despised disease seizes, squeezes one wheezy, woozy biddy.

'Tis tantamount to a figurative noose.

Debilitating, devastating, its viciously constricting grip
inexorably tightens.

The wreathing, writhing knot twists inextricably around her
neck, next to nixes this brittle, little lady's tenuous
existence.

Breathing decreases, ceases, as she deceases.

Mark Lyndon is a retired teacher, performance poet/singer from Swansea who runs events for local writers. He appears in an international anthology and has had two poetry books published. Ironically, his poem, 'Virus Versus Us,' was inspired by the dispiriting prospect of contending with an unseen enemy.

Overhead

Douglas John Imbrogno – Huntington, West Virginia, USA

1.

'The clouds don't care,'
he said, blowing a puff
of cigar smoke at me

from across the porch.
I sent a pretty good
smoke ring back his way.

It broke up three feet from
my lips. We were not
six feet apart, so could

be killing each other, should
the virus hitch a ride upon
our exhalations. Mine from

Honduras, his from Cuba
(he'd scored a Cohiba from
somewhere). He'd busted

out of quarantine. Had to
'*Get out of Dodge*.' Drove the
50 miles to my front porch.

2.

Ever since neighbor one, then,
neighbor two, felled ailing
trees of some height on the

cul-de-sac the last three
years, my view of clouds have
improved. I like to sit on the

porch when rain rides
west to east, and clouds the
shade of grapes and plums

roll like tumbleweeds
across the sky. When the
rain falls, my ears pick out

a half-dozen sorts
of sound. The initial patter like
cat footfalls in the house.

A more insistent splash,
like the whap of windshield
wipers beating time. Then,

the deluge, which never
lasts for long, but is a sight
to behold. And smell, when

thunderous ozone charges
new-washed air like static current,
crackling in flung

wool blankets on the bed.
"What do you mean?" I ask,
tapping off a toenail's length

of ash into a white Berea
Chamber of Commerce ashtray.
It might have been my

father-in-law's, before he gave
up smokes three years before he
died. "The clouds," he says,

"don't care about all this."
Points the Cohiba toward the
cul-de-sac.

3.

Neighbor Lavinia's golden SUV.
Craig's lawn, well-manicured as an
actor's beard. He put up a Trump sign

last election, surprising us. We
thought he wasn't one of those.
They'd sheltered our first kid the

night our second was born. He
and his wife would feed our cats
when we'd leave town. Before

they resigned, with a polite
but simple note: *'Our
cat-sitting days are done...'*

"We get sick, we die. Trump wins
again. We off a million species
in a hundred years," my friend says.

He taps an inch of ash into his
ashtray, a green glass one, its
provenance unknown to me. "The

clouds don't care," he says.
I look up at them. A big one holds
its shape — a herd of wild horses.

Five seconds later, just a charcoal
Rorschach blot above our heads this
cold late-winter day. It's almost too

cool to be on the porch. He sips his
Diet Coke. I draw a swallow of a
kombucha which tastes like root beer,

although not quite. "I should be
going. I need to pick up take-out
on my way." Take-out, for the moment,

is the only option. After he's gone,
I swig the last liquid in my bottle,
clouds tumbling overhead.

Douglas John Imbrogno is a lifetime storyteller in words and images. He worked three decades as a writer, editor and multimedia producer for the Charleston Gazette *in West Virginia. In 2020, he founded the multimedia magazine, WestVirginiaVille.com, which presents feature, news and magazine-style stories through text, photography, and video.*

Gluttony, Corruption, and the Forgotten "Nonbeing": COVID-19 and the Nature of Our Government in South Africa

Thamsanqa D. Malinga – Johannesburg, Gauteng, South Africa

There is a tree by my street that cuts a dying figure, alone and with no hopefulness of life. It has been dealt a hard blow by the change in seasons. On top of that, it is squashed by boulders. I remember how not so long ago it was a home to a diversity of birds, and slowly it started to wither with leaves falling daily.

Often, I observed municipal workers raking and burning the fallen leaves, and still every day they fell. As it continued to dry up, the birds left in search of a better and greener tree, like politicians once the ballots are counted and the results are announced. Now this tree stands dry, and it's unbearable to imagine it coming back to life, ever.

Earlier this year, COVID was just a virus outside our borders and our continent. Life was a bliss—but then we had one case of infection and the numbers went up. Well, they were below ten, but as they began to escalate, we went on lockdown for the touted 'readiness' plan—which gave us some form of comfort.

The recent snowball of infections made me reflect on this lonely tree dropping leaves at every chance of an autumn breeze. Then followed the cases of people succumbing, but as time has shown us, these deaths were no longer just 'cases' or numbers. They were not just leaves falling off a tree because it's autumn. They had names and faces. They were mothers, fathers, friends, colleagues, relatives. We lost relatives and close friends. I remember waking up to see a funeral of a friend on Facebook—I didn't even know he had passed on. Like a leaf off a tree, he was blown off the face of the Earth.

Going back to the tree on my street, and to paint a more vivid picture, at its peak, this tree grew big and green and stretched to the adjacent road to an extent that buses would scratch against it as they drove by. It provided shelter for birds and a cooling shadow to those escaping the scorching sun as they grew tired from the steep road leading to it. This tree was also faced with a struggle as it was nestled amongst boulders, a sign it survived more hardships within.

Lately, I have found myself wondering if these boulders, the harsh dry season, and migrating birds that had visited this tree, are not a reflection of how our leaders in government, the ruling party, and all in their midst are treating the COVID-19 pandemic.

The gluttony that surfaced from the pilferage of COVID relief funds, as well as the seeming lack of a cohesive plan to deal with the health crisis as well as an economy that is shedding livelihoods, has just been too much to stomach and witness. What has happened to our consciousness? In fact, the question is, has our government and ruling party become so inhumane? Politicians with their friends and families have now become the boulders that rest heavily on this tree, throttling the little life that's left in it.

COVID deaths, the job losses, poverty, and unemployment of young, abled people have just been 'cases' and reduced to numbers by those in authority—instead of being named victims of a state that failed its people. Unlike that figurative biblical tree which is said to be "planted along a riverbank, with roots that reach deep into the water (and) not bothered by the heat or worried by long months of drought (its) leaves stay green, and (they) never stop producing fruit," our reality is not like that. Our reality is that the reference to 'cases' shows a state of forgotten 'non-beings' left in the periphery to undergo social death.

A couple of years back, when men on the Platinum Belt went on strike for a decent living wage, there was a call for "concomitant action." This call resulted in the greatest and saddest massacre in our post-democratic dispensation in South Africa. When the people in the villages of the Eastern Cape were engulfed by drought and famine, there was silence. At the height of femicide, unemployment, and other ills of social death, the country and its citizens alike found themselves in a state of being the stark dry tree stripped of its leaves by the autumn winds of leadership inefficiency and repressed by bouldering political bureaucracy and gluttony.

COVID has shown us the nature of our government and the condition of harshness it has consistently executed on people, especially Black people, time and time again. In a matter of a few months, our country became a shadow of its former self—like the lonely tree stripped of its being by the winter season. As citizens, we became leaves to be raked off and burned, our lives and livelihood going up in smoke and vanishing into thin air. In all this, the was no "concomitant action" or sign of a cohesive plan. What we saw was a frenzy by government ministers jostling for media space with half-baked plans. On the other side, the ruling party got comrades and relatives to "investigate" each other over the looting and gluttony. As if that is not claptrap at its best, their cronies and families continued to repress us, like the boulders around the tree, with their plundering.

For South Africa, COVID-19 has been a chainsaw that was cutting down the economic wellbeing of our country whilst at the same time shaking off the lives of people like leaves of a dying tree. Whilst all of this is happening, the lumberjacks that are the politically connected lined up to cut off the wood and sell it for profit.

As Mother Nature visited the Southern Africa region with her winter season which might (or might not have) exacerbated the COVID peak, she surely made some of us reflect on the nature of our government, the political elite, and the ruling party, on how easily they forget and cast citizenry to the state of 'non-being' as alluded to by Argentinian-Mexican philosopher Enrique Dussel and French philosopher, Franz Fanon.

We shall not lose hope. After the devastation of winter, Mother Nature also brings about spring. This social death we are seeing shall pass. We will find time to mourn those we love who were failed by the system. The curve will flatten and maybe, just maybe, those who fed off our livelihoods and the lives of our loved ones will be brought to book.

In the meantime, we live with the words of the fabled taxi marshal ringing in our ears as he is said to have shouted at passengers: "You cannot expect change, you need to bring change." Never again must we let our country be turned into the desolate figure that is a dying tree repressed by boulders and we become falling leaves that are just statistics or 'cases'.

Time will come for our 'concomitant' action as a people.

Thamsanqa Malinga is a Johannesburg-based Corporate Communications practitioner, blogger, social commentator, and author of BLAME ME ON APARTHEID - Colonialism, Apartheid and the legacy of Townships as a peripheral space for 'non-beings.'

(photograph on next page)

Photograph by Thamsanqa Malinga

The Time of the Virus

Reviva Schermbrucker – Cape Town, South Africa

without calling on the goodly antidepressant in the sky
who passes out sweets wrapped in verse
we are left with this:
how beauty is heightened in the time of the virus
still for a long while
hung on the hedge in the blue-sky gallery
a butterfly exhibits his startling wings
yellow spots exuberantly splattered on fear black
a friend spies a white-faced cat in a tree
we take these sights and bind them around our
heart-knocking selves
we mix our breath into the air of the wide world
to join in with it
to allow its rocking rhythm to soothe us

Reviva Schermbrucker *from South Africa is a children's author/illustrator and artist who has recently taken up writing poetry. "Somehow words and images are intertwined in my being and I can't choose one over the other for they are so fundamentally linked. They feel they come from the same source."*

Hope During a Pandemic

Adrian Huq (17 years old) – Derby, Connecticut, USA

August 2020

It's not news to anyone that these past months have been
    turbulent and difficult for the masses
From undocumented people to the poor and working classes
I'm thinking about the needs of the elderly people we've
    neglected
For the people who don't have health insurance and can't
    afford to get infected
And for people experiencing homelessness who are left
    unprotected

I mourn the disproportionate deaths of Black people from
    COVID
But it's nothing new that the evils of racism are morbid
We cannot go on with this continued police brutality
Both these crises continue to further Black and Brown
    mortality

This time has shown me that more than ever we need radical
    change
For reform that's intersectional and that's long-range
As a country we can't progress
Until our issues and past evils are addressed
No longer can we act like it's all working and pretend
To our destructive systems we must work to make amends

But why did we need a crisis for others to pay attention to
    struggles that have been there?
For people to recognize what's happening, want to do
    something, and actually care?

But despite the negativity, not all hope is lost

For the best of humanity comes without a cost
People from all backgrounds have come together to fight
And found a way to turn the wrongs into rights

Legal actions for furthering social justice are coming about
As organizers and activists continue to gather and shout
City leaders around the world are committing to a green
      recovery from the shutdown
Maybe this pivotal movement in history isn't something to
      make us frown

This year has shown more than ever our interconnectedness
      to one another
And put on display how much we need our family, friends,
      sisters, and brothers
From creating masks to distributing groceries, I'm happy
      with all the actions of care
Through mutual aid, volunteering, and donations, we've
      extended our hands to share
I hope the energy towards justice for marginalized
      communities will carry on forever
And it gives me hope on how far we can go if we all band
      together.

Adrian Huq (they/them) *is an activist and artist from Derby, Connecticut. They are currently attending their first year of college at Tufts University.*

Isolation Is a Gift

Jennifer Pratt-Walter – Vancouver, Washington, USA

Today as the sun lifts there are
not enough Alleluia words.
Outside the door, lilacs wrap me
in a shawl of sweetness.

The horse meets me with a nicker
of gladness. I open the gate and
she trots through clover alight with dew
that flies from her hoofs in tiny beacons.

The pink azalea shakes her sex-scented skirts.
Solomon's Seal offers its inverted wine flutes
beneath an atlas of new leaves.

A late owl croons goodbye to night
and the blue heron croaks back,
waving her wing-wands through the sky.

How the fern heads unroll is a symmetry
almost too perfect to bear.
All is precious in this moment.
You are precious. We are precious.
We need not regret separation for now.
Isolation on this Alleluia-morning is a gift.

Jennifer Pratt-Walter deeply feels a bond with Nature and an introvert's world. She is a freelance musician and square peg. She lives in beautiful Washington State on a small farm.

COVID-19: Novel Coronavirus

Ayana Zaman (10 years old) – Dhaka, Bangladesh

Ayana Zaman, age 10, is from Bangladesh. She says, "We are all suffering from the Coronavirus. That's why I drew this picture."

About the Editor

Sandy Tritt – Parkersburg, West Virginia, USA

Sandy Tritt is a writer, ghostwriter, editor, and speaker. The founder and CEO of Inspiration for Writers, Inc., an international editing and critiquing service for aspiring writers, she has edited hundreds of manuscripts (fiction, nonfiction, and scripts), and ghostwritten dozens more. The author of several books, including *From Laundry to Love* and *The PLAIN ENGLISH Writer's Workbook,* her short stories have received many awards and have appeared in various literary magazines.

Sandy is a past president of West Virginia Writers, Inc., the state's largest writing organization, and past president of the Ohio Valley Literary Group. She was the recipient of the 2002 Artsbridge Arts Award for Writing and the West Virginia Writers' 2008 J.U.G. (Just Uncommonly Good) Award for mentoring writers. Sandy taught creative writing for the Jackson County Board of Education and has given workshops at the Connecticut Fiction Fest (Meriden, Connecticut), West Virginia Writers Conference (Cedar Lakes, West Virginia), the Alabama Writers Conclave (Auburn, Alabama), the Appalachian Writers Association (Bristol, Tennessee), the Writer's Project Runway (Leesburg, Virginia), the Lewisburg Literary Festival, and for the West Virginia Division of Culture and History (Charleston, West Virginia)—among many local and regional workshops. Invite her to speak at your conference or workshop.

You may contact her at IFWeditors@gmail.com or visit her website at www.InspirationForWriters.com.

9 781954 455009